HARVESTING

DREAMS

*DEFYING THE ODDS TO ACHIEVE
THE AMERICAN DREAM*

ERICA ALFARO

BARKER ❷ JULES

BARKER ⊗ JULES®

HARVESTING DREAMS

All rights reserved. © 2022, by Erica Alfaro

First Edition. Published by BARKER & JULES®.

Paperback ISBN | 978-1-64789-788-8
Hardcover ISBN | 978-1-64789-789-5
eBook ISBN | 978-1-64789-790-1

Library of Congress Copyrights Control Number: 1-10813130031

Printed in the United States.

Cover photograph | Aldair Nathaniel Sánchez
Book cover design | BARKER & JULES®
Book interior layout by Jessica Vallejo | BARKER & JULES®

BARKER & JULES® and their affiliates are an imprint of BARKER & JULES, LLC.

BARKER & JULES, LLC
3776 Howard Hughes Pkwy 549, Las Vegas, NV 89169
barkerandjules.com

Dedication

To my grandparents, my parents, and my siblings

CONTENT

INTRODUCTION

Everything happened so quickly. In May 2019, reporters started arriving at my house every two hours. I had another few hundred likes on social media every five minutes. All because my graduation photo had gone viral overnight. My photo and my story were in the news all over the world. I was being featured on the front page of several newspapers. I couldn't understand how a picture of me dressed in a cap and gown, standing in a farm field next to my farm-working parents, could garner so much attention. In just a few days, I had booked a whole month of appointments to give speeches to big audiences. How was this possible?

One of the first conferences was held at a community college. I arrived early, with the care and punctuality of someone who is looking forward to a new adventure. As I walked through the conference room, I noticed that my graduation photo, accompanied by a short description of my life, had been placed in the center of each table. For someone who, just a few days before, had lived her entire existence in anonymity, this was surreal, to say the least! The auditorium was so dimly lit that it was difficult to recognize a face. I found an unoccupied chair and sat down, facing a young woman who was alone. She was holding my graduation photo in her hand and staring out across the auditorium.

"Can I sit with you?" I asked.

"Of course, you can!" she answered kindly. "Are you also here to see the girl?"

I took a sip from my glass of water, smiled and nodded my head. She reached over and placed the photo in my hands.

"My teacher told us a lot about her, and that's why I came to hear her. This girl's story came into my life . . . like a revelation. Thanks to her inspiration, I decided to leave an abusive relationship, and now I am more determined than ever to continue with my education."

Tears welled in my eyes as I tried to speak around the lump in my throat. "This girl is me."

At that moment, I understood. For the first time in my life, I was grateful for all the adversities that had come my way in the process of getting a higher education: growing up with limitations in a culture rooted in macho beliefs, being a teenage mother, experiencing domestic violence, depression, and all the insecurities of a first-generation college student. I had managed to overcome them all. After deciding to tell my story, I was able to inspire someone to make a change in their life, to continue with their studies, and, thus, I had made a difference. In that instant, I discovered that everything, absolutely everything, had been worth it.

This is the reason I decided to write this book. Because perhaps you are that person who needs to hear a story that gives you hope and inspires you to dream big. I will tell you how it all started and how I got here. Throughout these pages, you will walk through my life and my memories as I remember them, as they happened. Welcome to my world.

PART
1

PART
2

MY ORIGIN–
THE BEGINNING OF
EVERYTHING

To tell my story properly, we have to go back to the starting point. My origin, my childhood, my circumstances—because these are what shaped my personality. This is true for all of us. We are the result of what has happened to us over the course of our lives and what we decide to make of it. You could say that's what this story is all about.

My life, like anyone's, began with an encounter between my parents. My mother, Teresa Herrera, was from Oaxaca, and from an early age, she experienced the most unusual hardships. Her father was murdered in the mountains of Oaxaca. Although I don't know exactly what happened because it was a taboo subject in my family, I can imagine that my mother must have been scarred by it forever. After her father's death, she was abandoned by her mother, who remarried and never returned.

Mom lived with her grandmother and her aunts, growing up in a hut where there was no money to buy meat, where frying an egg was an unthinkable luxury, and where they ate only tortillas with salt. At the age of eight, she started working with her grandmother, rising before the sun to travel to the mountains to collect soil to make the clay pots they sold in the plaza. Mom would stop in front of the local school from outside the fence and watch the kids playing in the schoolyard. With the bag of soil in both of her hands, she would ask her grandmother why she couldn't go to school. Her grandmother would remind her that they didn't have the money to send her to school. Mom never learned to read or write.

Of the stories I've heard about my mother's childhood, very few were pleasant. She doesn't like to revisit her past very often. However, one story she shared started out pleasant: when her uncle bought her a little dress. She put it on in a hurry, full of excitement. It must have been one of the only nice things she had ever received in her short life, but her aunt forced her to take it off and said she didn't deserve it.

My mother never felt welcome in that house; instead, she felt despised and unloved. It is a well-known fact that our childhood is the first and most important stage of life and that our personality is strongly influenced by the affection we receive at that time. When my mother told me those stories, I came to understand that her hard character was forged from her earliest memories.

My father, Claudio Alfaro, was from the same town as my mom. As children, they crossed paths back and forth and knew each other by sight, but they didn't meet again until they had grown up. My dad was very young when his family decided to move to Tijuana. He lived through a lot of poverty. His father committed domestic violence against my dad's mother, with long episodes in which he would abandon them. That is why my dad had to work from a very young age.

Dad was nine years old when he started selling gum on the streets, as a lot of children had to do in Mexico to help their families. He had no shoes, and he always wanted to know what it would be like to have access to education. He would look at the children carrying their backpacks on their walk to school and imagine that he was one of them. He would look into the windows of the classrooms, watch the lessons, and imagine that, someday, he would be able to enjoy those same opportunities. I imagine him on the outside looking in, watching so many children studying and doing something he would never be able to do, to then find his reflection in the window disheveled and malnourished. That image is the living representation of my family history. Coming from the bottom and seeing progress and education from afar, like a promise of salvation.

At the age of fifteen, Dad courageously crossed over to the United States to work in the fields of Vista, California. It was there, a few years later, that he met my mother again and they fell in love.

Mom was seventeen when she decided to leave home and follow her uncle to the United States. It was as if destiny itself had fought to cross their paths again. He was that boy who dreamed of books full of knowledge, and she was that girl who dreamed of clean, beautiful dresses. Fate had taken them from the same remote village to the same American fields.

MY FIRST MEMORY: THE FIELDS

My father obtained his U.S. residency in 1987 under the Special Agricultural Workers (SAW) Act. Unfortunately, my mother was unable to take advantage of the program. Soon after they began forging their romance, my older brother, Luis, was born. At the end of the farming season and the onset of winter, it became difficult for my parents to find new jobs and keep up with the high cost of rent in the United States. While my dad already had his green card, my mom had to wait to get her immigration status settled. So, without any other options, they decided to return to Tijuana.

When they arrived back in Mexico, my mother discovered, to her surprise, that she was pregnant with me. Luis, had already been born in the United States with the future opportunities that this could bring him as a U.S. citizen. My mom wanted the same for me, but how could a pregnant woman risk everything to cross the border to give birth in another country?

My father's residency status did not guarantee that she would get hers on time or ever. She saw time passing, which filled her with anguish. She ultimately decided it would be worth the risk to secure a better life for me. My dad disagreed with her, as he thought it was too risky. Against my father's wishes, she left home one morning when she was eight months pregnant. Without looking back, she made it her mission to get to the United States. During my own gestation, I was already between Mexico and the United States, between those two worlds that have marked me so much and that have shaped my personality. While still in my mother's womb, in 1989, I crossed into the United States.

A week after our arrival, I was born in the central valley of Fresno, California, the city that was familiar to Mom and where her uncle was working at that time. My father and one-year-old brother joined us a couple of days later. My parents returned to work in the fields; they worked for hours on end under the sun. My mom took my brother and me to work with her. She would place a blanket on the ground for my brother to play on and carry me in a *rebozo*, a woven shawl. Imagining my mother working, taking care of my brother, and carrying me at the same time is a beautiful symbol to me. We became a complete family with three children at home when my little sister, Susy, was born.

My first memory, in fact, is of a golden sunrise. I was only four years old, but the memory is so vivid that it feels like it was yesterday. It was a cold morning; dawn was breaking. My siblings and I were in the back bed of my father's old Ford truck that had a camper shell. We were all covered with thick blankets, and I was sleeping in the middle. I got up, carefully stepped over my siblings, and witnessed the most beautiful sunrise out the back window. The rising sun sat upon the horizon, bringing with it hope and the promise of a new life. In the distance, I saw the silhouettes of my parents working in the vineyard.

For the first five years of my life, my parents followed the farming seasons in California. They picked grapes, oranges, strawberries, cotton, cucumbers, tomatoes—you name it. As soon as one job was finished, they drove to the next town for the next one. From those early years, I have memories that fill my soul. I will never forget the long road trips, my dad playing music and eating his sunflower seeds, and my mom packing fruit and bean burritos. While on the road, when we were lucky, Dad would make a quick stop at McDonald's and buy us a cheeseburger. It was quite a treat for us. He would gently unwrap the cheeseburgers halfway and give each of us one. My parents always made an effort to give us a respectable life, despite being humble.

When we were little, we often played in the fields while my parents worked. The fields are the metaphorical encounter between my roots, my culture, my parents' sacrifice for us, and their love for their children. A starting point from which to dream.

MOM'S DEPORTATION

Dad applied for Mom's residency, but since they were farm workers who constantly moved to different cities, they missed the first appointment letter from the U.S Citizenship and Immigration Services (USCIS). Since they missed their scheduled interview without notifying USCIS within one year, their case was closed, and they had to re-apply. After a long wait, they were able to obtain the immigration interview. My mother was nervous about her appointment; she couldn't stop thinking about us and our future. My brother had just started kindergarten, and I was in preschool. My sister stayed with a babysitter so that both my parents could go to the appointment.

The wait was long and tedious; so many people were waiting for their appointments. Every minute that passed made Mom more nervous. When her name was finally called, she quickly stood up and followed the immigration officer into an office. Then, without any explanation and no empathy, the officer took her application and tore it up in front of her. She was stunned. They didn't let her speak; they just told her, "Your case has been denied. We are going to deport you today!"

Dad was in the waiting room when an immigration officer gave him the bad news. He didn't get to comfort Mom. He wasn't given the opportunity to talk to her, to assure her that we were going to be fine. After all my parents had fought through to be able to live with their children in the United States, to have my mother deported in such a way was unfair. At my young age, I didn't know that this was the bleak reality for so many immigrants.

That day, Dad picked us up early from school and then rushed to pick up my sister. The three of us sat in the passenger seat of his truck. We were all asking for Mom. He didn't answer our questions, perhaps because he was submerged in his thoughts or didn't know how to tell us. He left us wondering and just kept driving. As soon as we got to our apartment, Dad started pacing back and forth. His frustration rubbed off on us, and we began to cry. Then, without warning, he told us to grab whatever we could and that we were going to Mexico. Dad assured us that we were going to see Mom soon. The only thing I was able to take with me from the United States, as a magical treasure to keep, was my little radio with a microphone.

We returned to Tijuana full of uncertainty, thousands of dreams gone. The situation was frustrating because my siblings and I had U.S. citizenship and my dad had legalized residency, so the only one who was in the process of arranging her immigration status was my mom. But her application was denied because she missed the first appointment. So, my dad decided that we would all go with her to Tijuana while he looked for a lawyer to fight her case. He loved her so much that his concern for her was greater than the need for stability. Their union was true love.

When I left Fresno and entered Mexico in 1995, my childlike mind saw the world transform.

My first impression was strange. As you enter Tijuana, you can see mountains dotted with little houses, people selling candy on the street, and little children begging for money. Splendor was conspicuously absent in Tijuana. I remember thinking that I wished we had stayed in the United States. So many changes in such a short time. Besides, in a child's mind, changes are difficult to digest. Although, at the same time, the innocence and ignorance of childhood sped up the process. With nowhere to stay, we went to my grandparents' house. Oh, my grandparents! Let me tell you a little bit about them.

MY GRANDPARENTS AND THEIR CUSTOMS

Upon entering Mexico, my father left us with his parents and went to Mexicali to wait for my mother to be deported. When I saw my grandparents for the first time, they appeared as opposites. My grandpa, Jose, was cheerful—he received us with a wide smile, showing perfect teeth. He was very talkative, and his energy was contagious. Grandpa wore brown boots, a white dress shirt, and a white hat that had a peacock feather on one side.

On the other hand, my grandma, Regina, was quiet. She was more reserved and soft-spoken. I remember her tender face; she looked at us with so much love. She was wearing a gray *rebozo*, a white blouse, and a long pink skirt. They both spoke the Mixteco dialect, but only Grandpa could speak Spanish. Their warmth welcomed us and cut through the fear we carried with us.

My parents attempted to make the best out of that desolate situation and convinced themselves that this could be a new beginning, an opportunity to strengthen family ties. We lived with my grandparents for two years. Every morning during that time, my brother, sister, and I competed to be the first to say good morning and good night to them. That house was soon filled with the innocence that my siblings and I carried. Music always flooded out of the house, which seemed like a living radio at times. Grandpa danced in the middle of the living room, and we danced with him. His enthusiasm was contagious. He used to say that the singer Vicente Fernandez was his compadre, and I swore it was true. He loved to listen to music while Grandma cooked. Oh, I can still smell her food! It was delicious, and her *atole*, a traditional hot beverage, was the best.

My grandmother always spoke to us in Mixteco, and we understood her, even though we answered in Spanish. Curiously, she understood us. That's how we communicated. The only thing we learned to say in Mixteco is: *"Nai mei cuni ndoi,"* which meant, "Grandma, we love you very much." That was enough, because an "I love you" can carry in its words the whole heart. She would hug us back and say, "I love you too, grandchildren."

Every weekend, my dad and his brothers would gather in the back yard and listen to regional Mexican music while drinking beer around a campfire. We had left the United States and returned to Mexico to immerse ourselves in its customs and traditions. I was beginning to forge emotional ties with Mexico, although inside, I also felt American.

At home, my grandmother, my mother, and my aunts cleaned and cooked. It seemed like none of the women questioned whether that was their mission or not; it was established within our society. I was always getting in trouble for questioning why we couldn't be outside enjoying the campfire or why I couldn't have the same toys as my brother. When we received gifts, my brother got a soccer ball while my sister and I got a mop and a broom. I never saw that as fair. It seems incomprehensible to me now that a child can experience machismo but is not really able to understand it. My sister and I loved playing soccer with my brother, but my grandfather would always tell us that we were girls and shouldn't do that. He used to say that girls must learn to take care of the house and be obedient.

My grandmother got up early to make breakfast and wash all the clothes by hand. My grandfather waited to be served at the table and would get upset if my grandmother forgot to give him a spoon. He would scold her and make her do a thousand things. Although my grandfather was tender and affectionate with his grandchildren, he kept my grandmother in a submissive position. How could a man so candid with us be so severe with his wife? His old beliefs and traditions that he had learned in childhood trapped him in pillars that were difficult to knock down.

Mom told me the story of my grandparents, which was normal for them but seems crazy to me today. They got married when they were thirteen years old! My grandfather was playing marbles when my great-grandparents saw my grandmother in a square and told her parents she was very pretty. Without much thought, they went to ask for her hand—this was seen as a great honor—and her parents accepted. It was a time when your parents chose how you would live your life, your marriage, and your worldview. Of course, my grandmother cried and cried. She refused to get married, but she had to resign herself to the fact that it was going to happen against her will, and he, in turn, resented her because he didn't know her.

I can imagine my grandmother, a little girl who didn't even know what love was, much less sex or commitment to a partner, crying in the grip of her destiny, wanting to play with dolls while her aunts prepared her bridal veil. Who wants to get married at thirteen? No one wondered about the girl's feelings; in that day and age, such questions weren't taken into account. Her parents sealed her fate without her being able to grow up freely and choose her own path. My grandparents got married and began a life together that lasted until the end of their days. My grandfather committed domestic violence against my grandmother, with long episodes in which he would leave and abandon her and their children. When my grandfather would come home, drunk and full of rage, the situation got worse.

My grandmother resigned herself to that life as if it were her destiny. She accepted the role of a woman who receives such mistreatment because she thought that was what she had to do. How do you reinvent your world if it is built on such a solid foundation? What seems inconceivable to us now was, in those days, the norm.

Even though he was a macho man, I never observed violence within him; he never burst in anger, much less hit my grandmother. It is as if, when he met his grandchildren in his old age, he put aside his darkest parts and wanted to recover the illusion and magic. My memories of him are of a loving grandfather. There were times when he looked at us with so much love that tears came to his eyes. He always told us that he loved us very much and that we were his favorite grandchildren. He adored all three of us, but he always looked at my brother with more pride because he was the boy. All my life, I wanted Grandpa to see that I could be as strong as a boy. One day, Grandpa told me that Luis was the second man in the house. The conversation went like this:

"You have to obey him, Erica. He has the right to hit you," he told me.
"If my brother hits me, I'll hit him back, *Abuelito*," I replied.

Despite my young age, I understood that what Grandpa was saying was completely wrong!

My response took him by surprise. For a few seconds, he was silent. Then, slowly, a smile dawned on his face that hinted he was proud on the inside.

"Oh, granddaughter!" he said, shaking his head from one side to the other.

I always loved my grandparents; they were the most beautiful thing in my childhood. From them, we received a lot of affection, but we also learned ancient customs and beliefs. After two years of living with my grandparents, my parents had saved enough money and were able to buy a small house. The time had come to leave my grandparents' warm home behind, to get out of the comfort found there and move forward to make our own life.

A HUMBLE AND BEAUTIFUL CHILDHOOD

We were so comfortable and happy with our grandparents that we wished we could keep living with them. Their absence weighed heavily on us in the new house, even though we were still in the same neighborhood. After we moved, we always wanted to visit them, but Mom told us that we had to get used to being just the five of us.

The little house we moved into was extremely humble. It was built of wood and painted pale pink, but it felt dead. The floor was dirt, and the walls had holes in them. Everything was old, and we constantly had the feeling that the house would collapse at any moment. When it rained, there was always a puddle of water (if not a lake) in the living room. The bathroom, a shack with no light, was a pit toilet outside with a hole so big we had to be careful not to fall in. We bathed with cold water in a brown plastic tub that we put in the middle of the living room. The house had two rooms that were divided by a thin piece of wood—my parents in one room and the three of us in the other. Although we were never short of food, there was no variety. We ate mostly rice, beans, and soup.

My parents didn't have enough money to celebrate our birthdays; instead, they would buy us a pair of shoes and four sets of clothes. They never bought us a costume to go trick-or-treating on Halloween. We never had a Christmas tree or gifts to unwrap. However, we didn't know we were poor—we didn't know what we missed because we were around people who grew up the same way. The world was the one that appeared before our eyes. We took care of the things we had as if they were the only things on earth. We lived our childhood to the fullest: we explored the neighborhood, made little dirt roads, and created a little city that extended beyond our house. We were so happy! We found freedom in playing with other children. We were children, enjoying ourselves as only children can.

Dad worked in the United States since he was the only one with a green card. Every day, he crossed the border to go to work in the fields while Mom took care of us. Every Friday, Dad gave each of us two dollars. We would go to the store and buy chips and a soda that came in a bag with a straw. Mom was totally devoted to us, her many chores, and Dad. She dedicated all of her time and energy to taking care of others.

My mother washed all our clothes and dishes by hand in a *lavadero*, a concrete washing station outside the house. It seems unthinkable nowadays with all the technology we live with, and it wasn't that long ago! We lived in a traditional way. My mother performed the role expected of a woman, and my father that of a man. Unlike my grandfather, my father never assaulted my mother; he didn't follow in his own father's footsteps, who was negligent and abusive.

I have no memories of my parents being affectionate and loving toward each other; they never kissed or hugged in front of us. My parents both grew up without love, so they didn't know how to express it to each other or to us, but we knew they loved us. Love is an invisible force so powerful that it does not have to be demonstrated at all times to be felt.

Dad gave the same attention to the three of us. He was a patient father who showed his love with actions and never with words. On the other hand, my mother was strict and often scolded us. She was very marked by her hard childhood and sometimes gave us the same treatment she had been raised with, although we never missed the plate of food on the table. She always took good care of us.

My siblings and I got along, even though we had different personalities. My sister, Susy, was a shy little girl who preferred to stay inside the house and play alone. My brother could spend hours alone playing with his little cars in the back yard. I was a social butterfly who would often gather all the kids in the neighborhood to play with me. That would usually get me in trouble.

One afternoon, while playing with my siblings, I climbed my mom's fig tree and jumped to the biggest branch. The branch couldn't hold my weight and broke. When the broken branch was found, my mom got furious. She took my siblings and me to her bedroom and asked who was responsible for the broken branch. Nobody spoke up! In the silence, she pulled out a ladle and threatened to hit the three of us. She repeated the question. My siblings knew we were in for a beating, but they still kept quiet. They didn't tell on me, and that meant a lot to me. Luis, Susy, and I never snitched on each other. We always protected one another.

In my mental collection of beautiful moments, I remember one day when my mother appeared with a box that seemed to be alive: it made cute little sounds, and it moved around! The three of us approached her full of curiosity. It didn't take us long to open it. We were full of excitement to meet our first puppy, whom we named Oso. My siblings and I had always wanted a puppy. A neighbor's dog had had puppies, and she gave one to my mom. We loved him from the first moment he became a member of the family. Oso always gave us affection in times when we felt lonely. Since then, animals have represented love and loyalty to me. It was the most beautiful moment of my childhood; Oso was the best gift Mom could have given us.

My childhood was very humble, but I remember it with great happiness. Perhaps I was not weighed down for all the things I missed out on for lack of money because I couldn't yearn for what I'd never had. We didn't need more, and we didn't feel deprived. We were grateful for what we had, and that's how we were happy.

THE TORTOISE CAN
WIN THE RACE

While Dad worked in the United States, we went to elementary school in Tijuana. My sister and I wore brown skirts and white polo shirts for our uniforms. Although we lived a modest life, my mom always made sure we were bathed, combed, and fed. Since the schools in Mexico do not provide free food for students, Mom brought us lunch every day: flour tortillas with beans. She was always accompanied by Oso. We waited excitedly to see him, and he was also very excited to see us.

At home, my brother was ahead of me in every area. He was smart, and I was not as bright as he was, so eventually, insecurities began to grow within me. I would say to myself: "You are not worth as much as your brother. You are inferior because you are a girl. You will never achieve high grades in school."

When I was in 5th grade, I told my dad that I was very frustrated with my low grades.

"Don't worry, Erica," he said. "You're a little turtle."
"What?" I answered. "What do you mean, I'm a little turtle?" Turtles were very slow, but what did that have to do with me?

"You see, Erica," he said, "I'm going to tell you the story of the hare and the tortoise. It is the story of a tortoise whose shell was heavy, so it walked slowly, and a hare who ran fast. The hare mocked the tortoise for his slowness, and to humiliate the tortoise, he challenged him to a race. The tortoise accepted the challenge without letting the hare intimidate him. The next day, at the starting gun, the race began. The tortoise went steadily at a slow pace while the hare ran around the tortoise in a mocking manner. Afterward, the hare decided to take a nap, confident that the tortoise could never beat him. By the time the hare woke up, he noticed that the tortoise was already just a few steps away from winning. The hare ran as fast as he could, but it was impossible to catch up, and he had to watch the tortoise win the race."

My dad looked at me straight in the eyes, full of sweetness, and said, "You see, *mija*, it doesn't matter if you go slow. The important thing is that you don't stop." With that message, I understood that my dad believed in me. The lesson I learned from that is that in life, you have to be humble and keep in mind that goals are achieved with patience, dedication, and perseverance. It is better to go slowly but at a steady and sure pace.

I always carried the little radio that I had brought with me when we came to Mexico; it was my precious treasure. What made my radio even more special was its yellow microphone. Besides the radio, Dad bought me a cassette of the superstar Selena Quintanilla, who I always admired for her charisma, her beauty, and her strength. "Como la Flor" was my favorite song. Like Selena, I had my audience! I loved to gather my stuffed animals and sing to them with my microphone as if I were at a concert. I arranged all my stuffed animals around me and read the positive phrases that I wrote in my notebook. I wanted to motivate my stuffed animals, which in turn served to motivate me. I told them everything that I really wanted to hear from someone else's mouth. I have always felt a lot of emotional connection with my teddy bears, even to this day. My little radio gave me so many fun moments! I was able to travel without moving! At that age, a toy can unfold an entire universe.

At school, it was easy to get distracted in class. The classroom had large windows, and I enjoyed watching the birds. For Mother's Day Carnival, the teacher asked the class who wanted to recite a poem in front of the entire school. No one raised their hand. Then she asked the smartest girl in the class if she could do it, but she refused. I was very curious to know what it felt like to speak in front of an audience. So, I plucked up my courage and raised my hand, determined. She completely ignored me. But no one else raised their hand, and she finally responded when she saw my insistence.

"But are you sure you're going to be able to memorize it, Erica?"

"Of course," I answered, feeling her distrust was very cold.

"I don't think you can memorize it," she said.

When I'm told I can't do something, it challenges me to want to do it even more. In the end, seeing that no one else wanted to do it, she had no choice but to give it to me. It was a full-page, quite a challenge for a little girl. If the teacher didn't believe in me, then I had to be the one to believe in myself. I practiced day and night. I put so much persistence into it that I memorized it word for word.

The day came, and I was about to stand in front of the whole school with a real microphone in my hands. I was wearing a white dress and had a rose tucked behind each ear. As I walked onto the stage, my legs started shaking. I was terrified. That was the first time in my life that I felt extremely nervous. I was about to tell the teacher that I couldn't do it, that I wasn't able to memorize it, but suddenly, I saw my mother in the middle of the audience, and I started to recite the poem. I remember everyone smiling as each word came out of my mouth perfectly.

"Dear Mother, adored mother . . ."

As soon as I finished the poem, everyone began to clap. The teacher, of course, couldn't believe it! Like the tortoise, I had proved her wrong, but more than anything, I had proved to myself that I was capable of overcoming my fears.

A few days later, my parents gave us the news that mom had finally obtained her residency. Ever since my mom was deported, my dad had been working with a lawyer to get her papers processed. After several years of effort and endless paperwork, he was able to get them approved. He made it happen! My parents were thrilled. That day they told us that Mom was going to start working and that we would be studying in the United States. Everything indicated a big change for the better: a new life.

A BORDER LINE

After obtaining her residency, Mom went back to work in the fields and enrolled us in San Ysidro Middle School. She had held onto the vision that her children would study in the United States, and now she was finally fulfilling that dream. I was eleven years old when we began to cross the border every day to go to school. We woke up every morning before sunrise, at five o'clock, so that we could be on time for our classes that started at eight o'clock.

While we lined up to cross, my parents would give a few coins to the children begging for money. Each one of them reminded Dad of his childhood. My parents always tried to help others in need, but there were too many children to help. It was perhaps my first real dose of reality. We attentively listened when Dad shared stories about his childhood. We felt fortunate to have our parents and that we didn't have to go through what Dad had gone through.

As soon as we got closer to the checkpoint, and it was our turn to show our documents, Dad would become very nervous, especially if the immigration officer was white. Even though my parents were already residents and were legally permitted to cross into the United States and work, they always felt intimidated. Unconsciously, we also learned to feel intimidated and experience the same anxiety. But every day, we crossed over and chased our dreams.

My parents dropped us off at school at six in the morning, so we were always the first students to arrive. After school, we waited for them at a nearby community center. It was an incredibly long day. We would play on the computers until they picked us up, usually at six in the evening.

I will never forget the first parent-teacher meeting. My parents arrived with their clothes full of dirt, inevitable signatures from working in the fields. My classmates' parents, however, were in clean clothes. It was a stark contrast, the kind that made you aware of an obvious difference. Mom and Dad sat in the back of the room, trying hard not to be seen. The teacher handed out a questionnaire to all the parents and asked them to write down their goals for that school year. My parents exchanged glances and started talking to each other in their Mixteco dialect.

I could hear the turn of heads—this heavy whoosh—and even feel the fixed gazes, like heated rays of light, when the other parents and my classmates stared at us. In front of everyone, my teacher asked my dad why he hadn't filled out the questionnaire. Her voice punctured the silent hall, carrying over to where we were. Dad's seat groaned as he squirmed with unease, and with great shame, he bowed his head and told her that he couldn't read or write. I could see the sadness and embarrassment on his face. This was the first time that I realized that Dad was illiterate. I felt so helpless to see my father feeling so insecure and uncomfortable, carrying with him a whole childhood without education and a life of few resources. That was the last time Mom and Dad went to a parent-teacher conference.

It was very important to my parents that we study and take advantage of the opportunities they had been deprived of. They enrolled the three of us in school, even though it went against their family customs. On many occasions, I heard arguments between my father and grandfather, who disagreed with my parents' decisions in educating their daughters.

My grandfather tried to convince my dad that my sister and I shouldn't go to school because we were girls. "The only one who has the right to go to school is Luis," I heard him say, "Luis is a boy. Erica and Susy are girls—don't invest in them. They will get married, and a man will take over. You'd better take them out of school." There is no doubt that my grandfather loved us, but he had his own beliefs. Customs that he had learned since childhood formed a strong foundation for his world views. It was very difficult to change his mind. My father didn't buckle; he refused to give in to his father's requests. The world was changing out there, and the winds of change were coming through the windows of our house.

On the morning of September 11, 2001, we crossed the border earlier than usual. My parents dropped us off at an acquaintance's apartment because it was not safe to be at school while still dark. My siblings and I sat in the living room watching TV. In horror and disbelief, we learned that a plane had crashed into one of the twin towers of the World Trade Center in New York City.

We were already walking to school when a second plane crashed into the second tower. We watched the news while we were in class. We saw the same scene hundreds of times that day, along with the rest of the planet. Chaos was shown as if it were an apocalyptic movie. We were terrified! All the teachers looked devastated, and many of them were crying outside of class. We began to see how the parents of other children came for them to take them home, to a safe place, but our parents never arrived. They couldn't; their jobs didn't allow it. The classrooms were almost empty, and we were still there waiting for them.

The following day, we woke up early again to go to school, but the world had changed. This tragic event had etched itself in history. The lanes to cross the border didn't move. My father started banging on the steering wheel.

"We aren't moving! I'm going to be late for work," he said.

No one had expected the events of September 11, or that our daily lives would be impacted by that tragic event. It became very difficult to cross the border each day. The lines were endless, and now we had to wake up at 3 a.m., much earlier than usual. But still, every day, we crossed the border to go to school. At the end of that school year, proof of residency was required to continue studying in the United States. My parents were determined that we would continue studying. The only way was if they rented an apartment in San Ysidro, so that's what they did. They had to ask their neighbors in Tijuana to watch over our little house and to take care of Oso, as the apartment didn't allow pets.

My parents rented a one-bedroom apartment only a few minutes away from school. We shared it with my uncle and his wife, who slept in the living room while my family slept in the bedroom. We didn't have to keep driving back and forth across the border anymore. We were happy that we no longer had to wake up before sunrise, and we had more free time to play with other kids. After living in that apartment for a year, the manager evicted us. She found out my uncle and his wife, who were not in the rental agreement, lived there.

My parents struggled to find a new apartment and decided to reach out to my mother's brother, who had lived in Oceanside, California, for many years. Uncle told us that there was an apartment available in his complex, and since we couldn't find a new apartment in San Ysidro, it seemed like the only option. Although my parents never had the opportunity to go to school, they knew the importance of having access to a good education; their biggest dream was for their children to study, as they knew that studies would open countless doors for us. Their daily struggle for us to have a dignified life is something I am still grateful for today.

So, we set off for another destination, to start from scratch again. What we didn't imagine was that the neighborhood that we were moving to was going to be a place worthy of an action movie, and not in the good sense.

PART
2

A NEW WORLD

Oceanside is known for its iconic wooden pier and wide sandy beaches. It's located just south of Camp Pendleton, the busiest military base in the United States. Like any other city, it's also divided into social classes. In some parts of the city, there are beautiful and luxurious homes that belong to the upper class.

We arrived at Crown Heights, a working-class neighborhood located less than one mile from the beach. It was the most densely populated area in the city, a six-block community where low-quality apartments were filled with people living together in crowded conditions. The streets were saturated with cars, and there was never anywhere to park.

We shared our two-bedroom apartment with another family and a couple. My family slept huddled together in one bedroom, the other family rented the second bedroom, and the couple stayed in the living room.

The walls were extremely thin, as if they were made of paper, so you could hear everything. If you lived downstairs, you could hear what was going on upstairs: the footsteps, the fights, the music. It was common to wake up in the morning in your shared bedroom with the rest of your family, open the door, and see people you didn't know sleeping in the living room.

The residents of that community were always on their feet, struggling to survive. Ladies passed by selling tamales, champurrados, bread, corn, and popsicles every morning, just like in Mexico. On every block, there were *loncheras*, stationary food trucks, which were like little shops.

The gang members knew the area as "Center Street", where street crime was common. Gangs and drug dealers congregated in the alleys. The sound of parties was unending, as were the sounds of drunks, gang members, fights, and police sirens.

We often ate dinner to the sound of gunshots and helicopters. It was common to go out on the street and have to run away because you heard shooting in the next alley. This was a life of danger, and it was inevitable that, at any moment, something would happen.

The stability in our house in Tijuana over the years had given way to a chaos that was new to us. It was a place where dreaming was an act of courage. It was very common to see teenage mothers with unplanned pregnancies due to a lack of resources. We had no role models and spent many hours alone and unsupervised. There were no professionals; all of the adults were either hard-working manual laborers or involved in crime. We didn't know anyone who had earned a university degree or had a job that required any amount of education. We had no idea that there was a different world outside our neighborhood.

One day, I was having dinner with my family and the people we shared the apartment with. The usual background noise of patrol-car sirens and helicopters looking for fugitives was all around outside. Suddenly, someone opened our apartment door and scared the hell out of us. It was a shirtless gang member with a bare torso full of tattoos. He was holding a gun in his hand. He closed the door and locked it. He demanded that we give him a shirt and told us not to make any noise. We were terrified! We didn't know how to react, so my dad gave him a shirt and a cap, and then the gang member sat there for a long time until the sirens stopped blaring. The scenario of a gangster movie, which seems like fiction to anyone else, was our harsh reality.

We were only an hour away from Tijuana, but it was very different. We missed our grandparents and Oso, and several times, we asked our parents when we would see them again. We were attached to them because we emotionally linked them to that oasis where we were so happy. It was hard to get used to the speed at which our lives were changing.

LINCOLN MIDDLE SCHOOL

Every morning, the kids in my neighborhood gathered together to wait for the bus that took us to Lincoln Middle School. I entered the English Learning Development (ELD) program, specifically designed for people who did not speak English. In my ELD class, all my classmates spoke only Spanish and, like me, they took most of the subjects in that language. To study properly or take extracurricular classes, I had to first learn English.

During the last week of school, we were taken on a field trip to California State University, San Marcos (CSUSM). I came to think of this day as the day that my life was divided into "before" and "after." The university was huge. Having grown up in a poor neighborhood in Tijuana where you only saw tiny wooden houses and dirt roads, the size of CSUSM was impressive and overwhelming. I had never seen such large and elegant buildings. I asked my classmate if it was a city, to which she replied, "This is a school where professionals are made: teachers, lawyers, and engineers."

I was speechless. Curiosity has always been part of my personality, a force that has kept my mind active, so even though our group was told not to split up during the field trip, I convinced my classmate to go explore this beautiful place. We headed off on an adventure! I opened the door to one room, and to my surprise, it was a huge auditorium. The teacher of that class invited us to sit down.

It was the first time I was surrounded by so many university students; I looked around the room, but none of those students looked like me. Most of them were white, and I began to feel intimidated. Was it possible that someone like me could study in this beautiful school? Like the wings of a butterfly that could lift me to a new world, a new universe was unfolding before my eyes. I, a Hispanic girl who could barely speak English, with low grades, who did not have the resources, could dream of a life so much more than anything I had been told I could aspire to.

Every birthday, my mother still bought us four changes of clothes that had to last the whole year, and that seemed normal to me. When I got home, I always washed my clothes and left them to dry overnight—normal, right? That's what everyone does! At least, that's what I thought until one day in the school cafeteria, some girls started looking at me and giggling. I was grabbing food with a friend. I greeted the girls, but my friend told me not to say hi to them.

"Why not?" I asked, surprised.
"No reason," she answered, as if trying to hide something.
"But tell me what's wrong!"
"They're making fun of you," she replied.
"Why?" I asked in shock.
"They're laughing at the fact that you always wear the same pants."

Yes, it was true, I had been wearing the same clothes for days and days; I only had the four changes of clothes that I'd received for my birthday. At that moment, I became aware of myself and began to contrast my clothes with others'. I saw that many did not repeat outfits and dressed well. It was an unwelcome revelation to see that this girl, with economic limitations, who cannot have an "all-inclusive" life like the others, was myself. That day changed my perspective of who I was in relation to the world. Something clicked in me. For the first time, I felt humiliated. For the first time in my life, I realized that I was poor.

I was fourteen years old and already beginning to realize that our way of living was not optimal. My parents worked all day, and we hardly saw them or spoke to them. When they came home from work, their clothes were full of dirt, and they had to get ready for the next day. Sometimes they even had to work seven days a week. They always looked tired, but they never complained. How could I ask them to take me shopping if they had neither money nor time? Then, I thought that if I told my mother I was being made fun of at school, she could do something about it. So, I told her I didn't want to keep wearing the same clothes every day.

"Do you know how much things cost, Erica?" she said.

"Yes, Mom," I answered, "I know. But I can't wear the same pants every day."

"What's the matter? Are they damaged?"

"No," I answered.

I wanted to tell her what had happened with those girls, but I did not dare. I had never talked to Mom about how I felt—I didn't know how.

"Look, Erica, that's all we can offer you," said my mother, looking me straight in the eye, trying to see beyond my childish self to the woman inside me who was beginning to grow up. "Now that your summer vacation is coming up, I'm going to take you to the fields so you can see how money is earned and what things cost." She always told us that things didn't fall from the sky. Things were earned with effort and sacrifice.

Mom wanted to teach me an important lesson. During that summer vacation, she took me to work in the fields. We arrived early, and there were already a lot of farm workers. At first, it didn't seem so hard, and I worked for hours picking and picking tomatoes without complaining. By midday, I felt I couldn't go on any longer. My back hurt and I was exhausted. In the distance, I could hear my mother asking me to hurry up.

"I can't take it anymore," I told her.

Mom put her arms on her hips as she spoke to me. "This is our life, your dad's and mine. We didn't have the opportunity to go to school. We don't have a choice. So, if this is not the life you want to have, you have to study."

At the time, I didn't know that this message from my mom would change my future and my life.

OCEANSIDE HIGH SCHOOL

Time was ticking away in Oceanside. By the time I turned fifteen, I was already a freshman at Oceanside High School (OHS). All the students who lived around the beach communities attended OHS, a thirty-acre-wide school with giant palms. It was only a six-minute walk from my apartment. The school mascot was a pirate that wore the same colors as the buildings: green, white, and black. Since we were close to the beach, the seagulls surrounded the school and waited patiently to take our lunch.

OHS was in the middle of two rival gangs, "Pozole" and "Center Street." Since it was common to see fights between those two gangs, security guards surrounded the school. During the lunch break, the gangs would gather in groups and stand at opposite entrances of the school. You had to be with a group of friends if you didn't want to be approached by one of them.

More than half of the students were Hispanic. Everyone segregated themselves: African Americans, whites, and Asians formed their own groups.

It was hard to make sense of things. What used to happen to me as a child, being blissfully ignorant, vanished. Now I realized that I lived on the complicated side of town in a place where you couldn't see opportunities. I had American citizenship, but I felt like an immigrant; I couldn't speak English, I didn't understand the new culture, I had left the place where I grew up—I felt lost.

One day, I skipped one of my classes and climbed to the top of the tallest tree behind the school gym. That's where I met my best friend, my dear Nallely. She was sitting on a branch, wearing headphones and listening to music with a CD player. As soon as she saw me, she removed her headphones and invited me to sit next to her.

"Hey, welcome to my secret spot!" she said with a smile.

"What are you doing here?" I asked.

"Like you—skipping class."

We both laughed.

There, we spent hours listening to music and talking. It became our meeting place. Nallely and I became inseparable. In addition to being best friends, we were therapists for each other. We had the sort of companionship that is so necessary when you are growing up. We lived in the same neighborhood; our living conditions were the same. Our upbringings were very similar, but there was a difference. Her parents were undocumented, and she lived in fear that they would be deported at any moment.

During this time, I didn't spend much time with my siblings. Our personalities and our interests were different. Luis started a soccer team with his friends; he spent hours playing in the park. Susy visited my aunt, who lived next door and watched novelas, Mexican soap operas. Meanwhile, Nallely and I walked around the pier or the neighborhood. We preferred to be anywhere but home. We all knew that we had to start heading home before our parents got home. That was usually around 6 p.m.

Every morning, Nallely, my cousin, and I would walk to school together. I was still in the ELD program, but now half of my classes were taught in English. It was taking me more than expected to learn that language, and, in the United States, if you don't speak English, it is difficult to flourish academically. I was very discouraged that I could not understand the required classes. My grades were terrible. I let my grades decide for me, wrongly giving them the power to rule my self-esteem.

My story took a turn when I met Hector, the person who came to change my life.

YOUNG LOVE

I met Hector in my second semester of high school, on the first day of class. Our ELD teacher was taking attendance. She called his name multiple times, when suddenly, the door opened and in strolled Hector, instantly breaking the ice with the silly way he walked in—he clearly wanted to make a humorous entrance to show off and grab everyone's attention. We all laughed at his bold audacity. He was carrying a skateboard in his hand and wearing a beanie, a white shirt, and blue jeans. He had a piercing in his right eyebrow.

He sat in front of me, waved hello, and smiled. I didn't smile back at him; instead, I turned away. He rested his head on his hand and stared at me without shame for the rest of class. I was amazed at how he didn't feel embarrassed at all. Our personalities were opposites: I was shy, while he was bold. The teacher moved him away from me several times, but he was very insistent and still tried to talk to me.

One day, he threw me a piece of paper from the other side of the room, asking me if I wanted to be his girlfriend, with the options "yes" and "no" written. I immediately circled the word "no" and threw it back at him. Even after that, he still pursued me! I couldn't understand it; Hector was a popular guy. He was so charismatic, the center of attention. He always had people following him or wanting to be around him. I was an insecure girl with few friends, short of affection, and who no one paid any attention to.

One weekend, I was in my living room with my cousin when a classmate called. Her brother was Hector's friend.

"Hello, Erica. We are in the same class. I have a mysterious person next to me who wants to talk to you," she said, and then she put Hector on the phone.

"I wanted to ask you something," he said straight out. "How can I get you to tell me that you want to be my girlfriend?"

At that moment, I put the phone down and whispered to my cousin, "Hector asked me if I want to be his girlfriend."

"Say yes," my cousin said. "Monday is Valentine's Day! He'll bring you a present."

I picked up the phone again and said yes. Just like that, I gave in without ever imagining that this decision would disrupt my life.

On Valentine's Day, he showed up with Goku-style hair, seemingly very confident. He handed me a purple gift bag and hugged me. I opened the bag and took out a blue stuffed animal that said, "I love you," when I squashed its belly. He gave me a card in the shape of a heart that said, "All my attention will be towards you." Suddenly, someone was looking at me; someone was paying attention to me, and little by little, I began to see him as a light in my life.

Shortly after we started dating, Hector dropped out of high school, and I began to skip classes to be with him. We saw each other daily. I was attracted to his personality; he always made me laugh. My parents didn't know I had a boyfriend, so I stayed home on the weekends that they didn't work. Nallely visited me those days while Hector would skate outside my apartment with his friends.

Four months into our relationship, he gave me an engagement ring as a promise of fidelity and love. We started working at the Del Mar Fair that summer, collecting garbage and cleaning toilets. We would sneak out to ride the rides and eat whatever the vendors at the fair gave us.

If a day passed when Hector didn't see me, he became anxious, always needing to know what I was doing. He could shift from delighted to depressed in seconds. I felt a lot of pity for him. He made me think that I was the only person he had. The day that I noticed cuts on his arm, he shared with me that he had started using drugs at the age of thirteen but stopped using them the day that I agreed to be his girlfriend.

Hector and I were heading out of work when a coworker approached me and gave me a stuffed animal. "Hey, I won this, but I don't want it." Then he walked away. A couple of minutes later, Hector pushed me against the wall without warning. He started choking me while accusing me of cheating on him. I was in shock! I barely managed to get away, ran to the closest restroom, and hid inside a stall. I stayed there for hours.

YOU ARE PREGNANT

Once the job at the fair ended, it was time to go back to school and start my sophomore year. After that episode, I was determined to end the relationship with Hector. His jealousy and excessive way of controlling suffocated me. At this point, I was at a stage where I wanted to be free to spend more time with my friend Nallely. I should have taken into account that Hector was a guy I had rejected several times; he didn't give up until he got a yes. I didn't see the red flags rising at his impertinent insistence. I should have recognized the danger.

For several days, I ignored all his calls, but I knew that sooner or later I had to confront him. On the day I was supposed to go to school and finally end the relationship, I fell asleep and didn't go. I was nauseous and thought maybe I was sick, but when Nallely arrived at my apartment and I told her about my symptoms, she asked me, "Could you be pregnant?"

My heart dropped at that question. The following morning, we skipped school and went to the clinic together. I arrived at the reception desk very confused. They had me fill out a questionnaire, which I completed with trembling fingers. They gave me a little plastic cup for a urine sample. Once that was done, the wait took forever. I prayed it was just a false alarm. *How could I have a baby? Me? At fifteen? Hector, a dad?* All I had been thinking about for the past few days was how to end the relationship. I was immersed in these thoughts when I heard the nurse call my name.

"Erica Alfaro, please come with me."

I stood up, carrying the weight of the whole world on my shoulders. It was as if I already knew the answer they were going to give me.

The nurse took me to a room that felt cold and lonely.

"Erica, the results are positive. You are pregnant."
As she said this, she looked at me with tenderness
and pity.

No way I'm pregnant, I thought to myself as my
stomach churned.

"How old are you, *mija*?" she asked me.
"Fifteen, ma'am," I said, my voice trembling.

The nurse handed me a flyer, then said, "You
have three options, Erica: abortion, adoption, or
continuation of the pregnancy."

I was in shock. I couldn't believe it—I was sure
they had made a mistake. It was simply not possible
that I was pregnant. I left the clinic in a sea of
doubt and emotional turbulence. I lifted my shirt
and looked at my flat belly. I caressed it, wondering
how it was possible that I was harboring life inside
me. But I was also thinking about myself, about my
future, wondering what I should do.

After leaving the clinic, Nallely and I walked
through the park.

"So, what are you going to do, Erica?" she asked me. "I don't know, Nallely."

Trying to make me feel better, she said, "Well, there are a lot of girls our age in the neighborhood with babies; it's not that strange."

We belonged to a community in which there was no sex education. In my house, it was a taboo subject. The only thing I was told about the loss of virginity was that a woman's value depended on her "purity". For men, it was different; their honor didn't rest on such a thing. I felt indecent about being pregnant. I felt guilty, as if I had done something terrible.

At our low socioeconomic level, the absence of sex education left my generation living in a precarious position as they tried to live life without the necessary knowledge. For instance, when my period first came, I got scared because I had never heard of menstruation. When I bled for the first time, I hid it from my mother; She never explained what it was.

On the way home, I crossed a playground. I amused myself by watching the children play, free, thinking that it wasn't so long ago that I had been like one of them. What's more, a massive part of me still felt like a child. I was submerged in my thoughts. Suddenly, a little boy about three years old came up to me and said, "Mommy, Mommy!" I saw that as a sign, and I still feel that way to this day. At that moment, I decided that the best option was to continue with the pregnancy.

After much thought, I called Hector and asked him to meet me outside of school. That afternoon, we sat on the sidewalk, and after a few minutes of silence, I finally dared to speak.

"I haven't been feeling well," I told him. "I've been nauseous, vomiting, and dizzy, so I went to the clinic to take a pregnancy test."

We looked at each other in a cutting silence.

"Well?" he asked, confused.
"I'm pregnant," I told him.

He was silent for a while. Little by little, a smile grew on his face. "Really?!"

"Yes," I said.

He stood up. "We're going to be parents!" he said, suddenly euphoric.

I think, in a way, he saw it as an opportunity to have something immense in common, like a child, and to have a definitive alliance between us. His eyes lit up, and his soul lit up, and that attitude rubbed off on me. I also began to look at this new stage with optimism, thinking that maybe Hector would change and everything could work out between us. But we were children; we were not ready. Due to my young age and inexperience, I didn't ask myself how he would treat our future son.

At home, I kept it a secret, but that secret exploded when the lady who rented a room in our apartment told my mom. Since she didn't work, she noticed that I wasn't going to school, that I slept all day and that I often went to the bathroom to vomit. As a classic gossipy lady, she asked my mother if she hadn't noticed that I was skipping classes and vomiting all day long.

So, my mother came up to me and asked, "Is it true that you are pregnant?"

I bowed my head. My mother read in my gesture a shy "yes" that encompassed an ocean of insecurities.

"Oh, Erica . . . You don't know the responsibility you have just gotten yourself into," she said while she put her hand softly on my belly.

I thought Mom would get furious, but instead, she looked devastated. I felt terrible for disappointing her.

Before introducing Hector to my parents, I asked him to remove his eyebrow piercing and cover his new tattoo. We all sat in the living room; Mom asked him many questions. When Hector told her that he didn't have his parents around and slept in a friend's living room, Mom felt pity for him.

Shortly after, Hector moved into our apartment. We slept in the living room. It didn't take him long to assault me again. Hector used force as a form of dominance. During the months of pregnancy, when my family wasn't around, I endured an abusive relationship. I was an abused woman, but I wasn't even that because I had not yet come of age, so I was practically a child who had grown up prematurely.

We were reproducing all the old patterns we had learned from the world around us. Hector was full of traumas, and he exerted those same traumas on me. Since I was expecting his child, I thought I had to stay with him, no matter what happened.

After every fight, Hector would come with flowers, sweet talk me, and swear that he would change. He manipulated me masterfully, coldly, making me feel guilty for anything. He was calculating, and I believed him.

Hector started a new job, and I started going to school every day. One day, I took an extra class after school. It was math tutoring because I was determined to improve my grades. Hector was waiting for me outside the school. When I came out, I saw him standing at the entrance.

"Why did you leave class so late?" he asked curtly.

"I am getting some tutoring to improve my grades. I want to finish high school." I was on the verge of stuttering. I didn't want to say something that would make him angrier. I could see in his eyes that he was on drugs, and my response was a shield to protect myself. He wanted to control my whole life while losing all control over his own.

"You don't have to go to school anymore; you have to stay home," he ordered me, making me remember the episodes when my grandfather and my father fought, producing in me great insecurity. I felt I had to submit to his words. What he wanted always came before any of my goals.

My mother always told me that my studies would open doors for me. At that moment, Hector boycotted that dream. All the sacrifices my parents had made so that their children would have a better future were annihilated by this episode. I dropped out of high school that day; I obeyed him.

THE HOUSE IN FRESNO

When I told my parents that I had decided to drop out of school, Mom tried to convince me to stay and finish high school, but I told her that I didn't see the point.

"I just want to focus on my baby," I responded.

I couldn't tell my parents that this was Hector's decision.

"You have no idea the sacrifices that your dad and I made so that you could get an education," Mom responded in a cold tone.

Then she continued by sharing how she was pregnant with me when she crossed the border. She reminded me of the days we crossed the border to go to school, the apartment they rented in San

Ysidro, and why we came to Oceanside. Dad tried to stop her when I began to cry, but Mom never held back her thoughts.

Grandpa was right, I thought.

My parents have always wanted the best for us, and now they were thinking about the stability of their future grandchildren. They had saved enough money, and they bought a house in Fresno, California, four hours north of Oceanside. With a baby on the way, me having dropped out of school, and Hector immersed in drugs and violence, we left for Fresno at the end of 2005.

At that stage, I no longer wore makeup or dressed up, and I had lost all of my friends. I didn't tell anyone what was going on with Hector. With his tyranny, he had turned me against my best friend, Nallely. I didn't even get to say goodbye to her.

On our way to Fresno, my parents drove behind us. As a result of an inferiority complex and competing to be the "man of the house," Hector became angry. "Why is your dad following us?"

he said to me cuttingly as he accelerated to pull further away.

"My dad wants to take care of us," I answered, giving an unnecessary explanation.
"I don't even want to go to Fresno with your family," he responded aggressively.

For the entire drive, he took it upon himself to make me feel that he was doing something huge for me. "Look what I'm doing for you! And on top of that," he shouted, "you won't appreciate it!"

I hoped that, after the birth of our baby, everything would change and that he would "heal", so to speak. He pronounced our son's name before he was born, full of illusion, and that filled me with hope. "Luisito," he would say, dazzled.

And I trusted the little ounces of innocence that still peeked through the cracks in his eyes. I was confident that the love that would be born for our baby would illuminate his path and dilute his aggressiveness. I clung to the few rays of sunshine I managed to see in him and truly believed that everything could change. I imagined us pushing the stroller in the park, talking to other parents, being good parents, having made it past all the bad times.

I blamed myself for all the aggression; I thought that maybe I could change things about myself so as not to make Hector angry. I thought that perhaps I was the one with the problem, that I could start to shut up more, not talk back, and agree with everything he said to avoid arguments.

A couple of weeks after arriving in Fresno, Dad accepted a good-paying job at a landscaping company that would require him to travel extensively. His first assignment was at Camp Pendleton, which meant my family had to go back to Oceanside. I never dared to tell them what was happening; Hector was only abusive behind closed doors.

The day my family left, the loneliness I felt was crushing. Now, it was just Hector and me. The house in Fresno was on the corner of East Thomas Avenue and Eighth Street. From my room, I could see a big lagoon and the main highway that could take me south, the direction that would return me home to my family. But Hector had locked me in his dark world, all for himself.

In Fresno, Hector couldn't hold down a single job. He was an absolute disaster. He always showed up at work late and stoned, and they would fire him quickly. On one occasion, I went with him to look for a new job. That bothered him a lot. On our way home, I suggested we collect cans to recycle and get some cash. I was desperate. But the solutions I offered were the object of his rage. It seemed that the mere fact that I thought and had a voice of my own drove him mad. I went out looking for cans to sell, pregnant, while he couldn't even work because of his drug addiction. Our lives were miserable.

One afternoon, I came home from picking up cans, and without warning, he started hitting me with all his might. He grabbed me and threw me to the floor, and as I fell, my stomach crashed against the corner of the bed. As if that wasn't enough, he sat on my stomach, unloading all his weight on it while he hit my head. He poured all his anger on me that day. He had never hit me like that before, with such vicious, brutal force.

I didn't cry or try to defend myself that day. I accepted his punishment, believing I had done something terrible. When you are assaulted like that, explanations are nonexistent. It is unjustifiable, and that is why your mind tends to look for a reason. You blame yourself for their violent acts, because the easiest thing is to believe it is your fault, that you provoked it, that you deserve it. That night, after this episode of violence, we went to sleep as if nothing had happened.

Just hours later, I woke up soaked in a pool of blood. Hector rushed me to the hospital.

LUISITO

Hector didn't stop at the stop signs; he passed all the traffic lights. We arrived at the hospital at 5 a.m. I heard other women crying in pain as I entered the delivery room. I asked Hector to call my parents. The nurse who took my pressure noticed the bruise on my arm. I told her and the doctors that I fell when I was going down the stairs.

The contractions started and got stronger and stronger, to the point that I thought I couldn't handle the pain any longer. My due date was March 31, a month and one week away. They gave me an epidural. We tried to make it a normal delivery for hours until I lost all my energy and passed out. When I woke up, my mom was standing next to my bed. "The doctors decided that a C-section was the best option," she said with a broken voice. She truly believed that I had simply fallen.

Hector's violence had caused me to go into labor a month early. Despite having a tremendous fright and a complicated delivery, when I held my baby in my arms for the first time, all the evils of the world melted away. I loved him immediately.

When my dad entered the room, he strolled toward Luisito. His eyes brimmed with tears, and without saying a word, he gently carried him.

"You're a grandpa, Claudio!" Mom said.
"We're grandparents," Dad responded with a smile. They both looked joyful.

My brother walked in and handed me a stuffed animal. Susy poked her head into the room and slowly walked in, and gave me the cheeseburger and candy she had sneaked in. Dad carefully handed her Luisito. Her excitement was so contagious that it rubbed off on Luisito, who gave her his first smile.

I was in the hospital for three days, my parents and siblings visited me every day. They stayed in Fresno for an entire week before returning to their lives. What I didn't know at that time was that my family had planned a baby shower for that weekend. It had to be canceled.

Suddenly, Hector seemed like someone else, someone incapable of attacking others. He caressed our baby, wrapped him in tenderness, and swore a new life, promising a new personality. We began an emotional honeymoon. We both took care of our child; Luisito represented joy in our house and flooded every corner with optimism. All our problems vanished. We put Luisito in between us in bed. We tickled him, and we laughed.

Hector stopped using drugs, started working, and brought home money. We had diapers and clothes for the baby. During that time, I was able to see his best parts, his glow. In his attempt to be a good father, to rescue his lost love for humanity and pour it on our son, I could see his best sides. It seemed like Hector had managed to break his past traumas as they were eclipsed by the happiness his son brought him. Had everything before been nothing more than a nightmare? Those few months were like an oasis. I was no longer studying, so I could devote myself to my son from sunrise to sunset and thus fulfill my task as a good wife while Hector worked.

They say that after the storm, the sun comes out. There are times in life when it is just the other way around: after a sunny day, without warning, comes the storm. And, after too many suspiciously sunny days in my life during that time, the storm returned. Hector started having tremors and a high fever. His body could no longer withstand such a long time without drugs.

One morning, I opened the bathroom door and found him getting high with his glass pipe. We looked at each other. I didn't say anything; I just closed the door and turned away. But I knew any chance for happiness had just disintegrated.

If you have met a drug addict, you know that the idea of living a dignified and normal life with that person is impossible. Not even before Luisito's birth, when I knew he was a daily drug user, had I ever seen him do it. Seeing him in that state, with the pipe, made me feel so sorry for him. It shocked me. At that moment, I discovered that the dream had been consumed, that everything would go back to the way it was before.

I went into the bedroom and hugged my baby. I stood there for a long time, frozen, my mind blank while Hector stayed in the bathroom getting high. I went to the window, and I looked at the highway heading south and wondered where all those people were going, why they were traveling while I stood in the middle of nowhere with my life ruined.

Remembering him shaking and crying from the drug withdrawals made me feel sad and helpless, and as much as he wanted to, he couldn't save himself. Much of his violence resided in his addictions. While this did not justify the violence, this component, along with the fact that he was a minor and very unaware of what he was doing, made me excuse him. At that moment, it was hard for me to see him as the abuser that he undeniably was. Hector wanted to be a good father, yes. He had tried, but he failed. It broke my heart just to think about it.

Every day, I sat in front of my window, patiently waiting for someone to rescue me. I always imagined that I was inside one of those cars on the highway, returning to my parents. I managed to free myself from his mistreatment in the small space that my imagination allowed me to recreate. I felt like a victim of life. Who was going to rescue me? I was depressed and lonely; I felt sorry for myself. I cursed my life. I was in a state of permanent victimhood.

I wanted things to change, but I didn't dare to even think about leaving the relationship. "I can't leave my son without a father," I repeated to myself every day. Sitting in front of my window, waiting for my life to change, became a daily routine. There I was, sixteen years old, living with an abusive boy who didn't understand life and who, wrapped in rage, took it out on me. So, that's what I did. I endured whatever came my way because I considered it my role. My example of a woman was that of my grandmother, who had resigned herself to her impending fate.

But one afternoon, everything changed. I was outside the house with Luisito in my arms, waiting for Hector to come home from work. I didn't have a car. Luisito needed diapers, and the only person who could take us to the store was Hector. As soon as he arrived, I told him to take us. Without waiting for him to respond, I opened the car's back door and quickly buckled Luisito into his seat, sat next to him, and closed the door.

Hector started the car so aggressively. From the back seat, I could see his red eyes. I became very concerned for my son's safety. I knew Hector was on drugs. He started driving faster and faster, ignoring all the red lights. I screamed at Hector to take me back home, to stop, at least for our son who was in the car. He made a quick U-turn and sped home. He was furious!

As soon as we arrived, I unbuckled my baby and tried to get him out of the car seat. Then Hector got out of the car, opened the back door, and tried to force me out, but I resisted. Unable to get me out of the vehicle, Hector turned toward the house. It seemed as if he had come up with an idea and ran inside. I didn't think twice. I took advantage of the moment and hugged Luisito, put him in the stroller, and fled.

He had endangered our lives, but above all, my son's life. I could bear him hurting me, but never my son. I hadn't expected that and understood it even less. Wasn't he supposed to adore him?

I wandered through the city, not knowing where to go, only knowing that I wanted to go far, far away. Then it got dark, and the temperature dropped significantly. I had no money and not enough warm clothes, and even though I panicked about going home, I thought it was the only alternative. It was official that my own home had become an unsafe place for my son and me. It had been that way for some time, but that was the day it hit me.

When I arrived home with Luisito, I realized no one was home, to my relief. The car was gone, Hector was gone, and the front door was wide open. I ran into the house with Luisito in my arms. I grabbed a sweater, changed his diaper as fast as I could, and packed the first things I could get into a plastic bag. I was ready to leave until I heard the engine of Hector's car. My heart started racing. I gathered my baby into my arms and tried to run out with the few things I had been able to grab, but it was too late. Hector was already at the door, blocking my way out. He snatched the bag from me and threw it inside the house. Then he grabbed my arm and forced me out into the street. With my baby in my arms, I begged him to let us sleep inside. Besides, the house belonged to my parents! He didn't have the right to stay inside and kick us out. But he locked all the doors and windows, so there was no way to get inside. I couldn't believe what was happening.

It was a cold and dark night. I had nowhere to go, so I sat in the corner of the house. The coldness gripped my body. I started shivering, but my only thought was to protect my nine-month-old baby. I removed my sweater, wrapped him, and pulled him closer to my body. Luisito fell asleep, and I let a torrent of desperate tears run down my cheeks until sleep finally overcame me. I was utterly sad; I had hit rock bottom.

Suddenly, in that dark place that I had reached in my mind, I could hear my mom's voice calling me in the distance, yelling, "Erica, *mija*, hurry up! You're falling behind." It was a vivid memory that came back in a dream, a memory of the summer vacation when she took me with her to work in a tomato field at age fourteen. We were in the middle of the field picking tomatoes. I could smell the earth, feel the wind brush against my face, see the stretch of green with dots of red popping around me. My mother's gaze was clear.

I remember that when I told her I was tired, she stopped and said, "This is our life. We didn't have the opportunity to go to school. We had no choice. If you want a better life, you have to study."

I opened my eyes just as dawn was breaking and the sun was rising. I saw my son's eyes—they were wide open. It was then that my "aha" moment crystalized, and I knew what I had to do. I held him close to me.

"Luisito," I vowed, looking into his eyes and gently kissing his forehead, "I promise I will go back to school, and no matter what it takes or how long it takes, I will get a good education, and I will change our lives!"

He must have felt my excitement because, even though he was so small and unable to understand what I was saying, I'm sure he connected with my heart, because he responded with a big smile.

PART
3

ANGELS ON MY PATH

As much as I wanted to run away, I had nowhere to go. As soon as Hector left for work that morning, I went inside the house. I decided that the best alternative at the moment was to go back to school and wait until I came of age. My main focus was to go back to school. Once inside, I searched around the room for change. I was able to collect six dollars. I packed a bologna sandwich and put my son in the stroller. I had no idea where to start, but I headed for downtown Fresno. After asking around for a charter school to study from home, I arrived at New Millennium High School.

I walked quickly to the admissions office and waited for my turn while the receptionist helped a Hispanic woman who was carrying a baby about the same age as Luisito. She was enrolling her teenage son. As soon as they left, I approached the front desk and told the receptionist that I wanted to enroll.

"You have to come with your parents; you can't enroll by yourself," she told me.
"They live in Tijuana, and they can't come right now," I answered.
"You are a minor; there is no way you can enroll if you don't have an adult, parent, or guardian coming with you," she said.

I was determined to enroll that day, but my parents were five hours away. I didn't know what to do until I remembered the woman who had gone before me. Without thinking twice, I caught up with her outside the office.

"I need your help," I told her in dismay. "They won't let me enroll without my parents. Can you please tell them that you are my mother?"
"I'm sorry, *mija*, but I don't want to get in trouble," she answered, confused.
"Please," I begged while holding Luisito. "I want to do it for him. I want to study to give him a better future."

My eyes grew hot—I was about to burst into tears. For the last few months, my life had been a pressure cooker that was just one degree away from exploding. She noticed my desperation and my pain.

"All right, let's go," she said while looking at Luisito.

We walked back to the office. "This is my mother, and she's going to help me enroll," I told the receptionist.

"What papers do I have to sign?" the Hispanic woman asked.

Just a few minutes before, I had told the receptionist that my parents lived in Tijuana, but she pretended that I hadn't told her. She looked behind her shoulder, hesitated for a second, and then decided to help me. She handed us the forms and helped us complete them. In the complicity of those two women, I found an immense love, even though they were strangers. I wouldn't be here today telling my story without those two women.

I went back to collecting cans, and with the money I made from that, I paid for the bus to go to school once a week. It was an independent-study program with individualized instruction. It was perfect because I could take Luisito with me; I could study and be a mother at the same time.

Once a week, I went to pick up assignments and submit my completed work. Hector didn't know anything because I hid this from him. One day, he found my homework under the bed. A big argument started when he found out; he tore all my hard work to shreds right in front of me. He was not just destroying my homework; he was also tearing my dreams into a thousand pieces.

"Do you really think you can finish high school? Look at you! You can't even speak English. You're just making a fool of yourself. I bet you anything that you won't make it." He didn't realize that, at that moment, he awakened the little girl who lived inside me, the little girl who didn't like to be challenged. At that moment, my biggest goal was to get a high school diploma and prove Hector wrong.

Hector wanted to see me fail miserably, and to prove his point, he allowed me to continue with school.

My parents were far away, and I was embarrassed to tell them about my situation. Even I was having trouble seeing the seriousness of the issue because I was so immersed in my own story. I didn't want to worry them. Although my mom called from time to time, I was alone, and living with someone like Hector made it hard to feel motivated. But when you want something and are willing to fight for it, life can sometimes work in your favor and put angels on your path. On this occasion, someone else appeared in my life to support me.

When you sign up for a charter, you receive one-on-one support from your assigned teacher. My assigned teacher was Mr. Lee, an African American man in his late sixties. He was very tall, wore glasses and had a wide smile. His tone of voice was thick, like a newscaster, yet cheerful and charismatic. He was very comical and endearing. He dressed professionally, elegantly. He didn't speak Spanish; he only spoke English. I understood everything he told me, but I could only answer with short sentences, as I still struggled to communicate in English.

In order to know which classes to assign me to, Mr. Lee requested my previous grades. I was embarrassed and nervous.

"Do you know something, Erica?" he said to me.
"Tell me, Mr. Lee."
"Don't be alarmed—these grades don't represent what you're worth, nor your intelligence. They just represent how hard you've worked in the past. Remember that what you put into life is what you get out of it. So, if you want better grades, you have to work harder, and you will get better results. I will help you; we will make a plan together. You will leave this school with a high school diploma."

Like the rest of the New Millennium Charter School students, I belonged to a low socioeconomic group full of limitations. I didn't have my parents around; the only person I had was Hector, and he abused me in every way. But now there was Mr. Lee, supporting me, believing in me, guiding my life.

Mr. Lee was a teacher who believed in the potential of his students—he truly wanted us to succeed. He gave us the attention and encouragement that we lacked. Mr. Lee was an angel who came into my life.

Once a week, I put Luisito in a kangaroo baby carrier and walked a couple of miles to catch the buses to school. One day, I was late for my meeting. It was summer, and it was over ninety degrees outside. Luisito and I were drenched in sweat.

"Who brings you to school?" asked Mr. Lee.
"I take two buses," I answered.
"Well, from now on, you won't have to do that," said Mr. Lee.

He offered to stop by my house during his lunchtime to pick up my completed homework and drop off new assignments, so I wouldn't have to go all the way to school.

At home, the conflicts with Hector grew. Sometimes, I wanted to leave everything and go to Tijuana with my parents, but I didn't want to disappoint Mr. Lee. I never told him about my situation, but I'm sure he could feel it. He would always remind me that I was only a couple of months away from graduation.

During my last week of high school, I stopped by to turn in my last assignment. Mr. Lee asked me if I was planning to go to college. I was stunned and didn't know how to react. For me, going to high school was already of incomparable merit, as my biggest goal was to get a high school diploma. College was never in my plans.

"Can someone like me go to college?" I asked through my thick accent.

"Of course, you can!" he answered as he grabbed a folder that had my grades. "Look; come and see. Your grades have improved a lot. They are very good. This proves that you are capable! Promise me that you will go to college, miss," said Mr. Lee, while looking straight into my eyes.

"I promise," I replied.

I left his classroom that day with a new goal: to go to college and return to my parents. I don't know what would have happened to me at that time without his support. There are times when you need someone from the outside to trust you and put in your sights ambitions you never even dreamed of so you can ask yourself, "What if I'm capable and I just don't know it?" Mr. Lee was the kind of person who knew how to see through our eyes more than we did ourselves.

So, finally, I finished high school. It was impressive for me to achieve it, having studied as a teenage mother, with Hector tearing up my homework and making comments that lowered my self-esteem. Finishing high school was one of the first times in my life that I felt proud of myself. It made me think I was capable of accomplishing anything I set my mind to.

On graduation day, all the New Millennium High School teachers lined up to shake our hands and hand us our diplomas. I was so excited; I ran to hug Mr. Lee. With a lump in my throat, I looked up and thanked him. He looked at me with pride, and I felt fulfilled. There were many things I would have liked to tell him, but at that moment, I still did not know how to express myself well in English. I wanted to tell him that I owed part of my diploma to him and that I would not have been able to achieve it without his support.

My parents and siblings traveled from Tijuana to Fresno to see me graduate. When I came down from the podium, Mom hugged me. She told me she was so proud that I had fulfilled her biggest dream. My mom, a woman I never saw cry in my childhood, cried with emotion. I was the first woman in her family to receive a high school diploma. The efforts had paid off, and the hard road had been worth it.

Hector attended the graduation ceremony, but he never said a word. As soon as we got home, I overheard him in the room talking to his mother over the phone. I wanted to share the good news with my mother-in-law, so I approached Hector and whispered, "Tell your mom that I graduated from high school," and he did.

"Erica graduated from high school today."

I put my ear on the back of the phone, thinking that she would be happy, but to my surprise, she got very upset.

"Why did you allow her to go back to school?! You have to make sure that she doesn't continue with her studies. She has to serve you and be a housewife." I walked out of the room and went back to the living room with my family. I wanted to enjoy the small celebration my parents had organized for me, but her words wouldn't get out of my mind.

I was determined to move back to Oceanside to be close to my family, so as soon as my family left, I convinced Hector that the best option was to return. I told him that I agreed with his mother and promised him that I would not continue my studies. He liked the idea, and we returned to Oceanside a couple of weeks later.

MY HEROES

I was eighteen years old when we finally moved back to Oceanside. I couldn't believe it. I had dreamed so many times of coming back. I brought with me all the clothes I had; three pairs of pants, three shirts, a sweater and a pair of flip-flops. I no longer wore makeup and only wore a long braid on my side.

My brother lived in Chula Vista; he was in his second year of community college. We rented a one-bedroom apartment, which we shared with my parents and my sister. Since the apartment only had one bedroom, Hector, Luisito, and I slept in the living room.

One afternoon, I was in the kitchen doing some chores when my brother Luis surprised us with a visit. Hector was in the shower, so he didn't hear my brother's arrival. My brother sat down in the living room, and at that moment, Hector came out of the bathroom very angry. I tried to tell him my brother was in the living room, but he didn't let me talk. He grabbed my arm and pushed me against the wall with great violence.

Luis quickly got up from the sofa, ran to him, and pushed him to the floor.

"Who the hell do you think you are to treat my sister like that, huh?"

Hector didn't know my brother was in the house, and he didn't expect that reaction from him. I have to admit that I didn't either.

"Let's see how brave you are. I dare you to hit me!" my brother said in a loud voice.

Hector looked scared and simply didn't react; he backed down.

It was the first time someone had defended me, that someone had stood up for me and stopped an episode of violence from my abuser.

My brother picked Luisito up from the floor and hurried us out of the house to his car.

"Why are you with him?" he asked me behind closed doors, isolated from the rest of the world. "I'm afraid. Besides, Hector is my son's father," I told him. I no longer had a sparkle in my eye, and I'm sure my brother no longer recognized me, so I lowered my gaze. I sensed sadness in his. "You are no longer alone. I promise I will take care of you," he said in a warm voice.

I was so used to this treatment and thought I deserved the abuse. It took my brother coming in, seeing it from the outside, and standing up for me to give me the wings I needed to fly away.

The straw that broke the camel's back happened a week after my brother defended me. I had bought a printer with the scholarship money I received after completing the enrollment process at the community college. For no reason, and with no provocation, Hector broke it. He smashed it in front of me and then hit me.

This gave me the strength to end my relationship with Hector. The following day, I packed Hector's clothes in trash bags and put them outside the apartment while he was at work. When he came home, far from the violent reaction I had imagined, he looked remorseful.

"But what did I do to you, may I ask? Everything is going well. I'm working, and we hardly argue."
"And what about the printer you broke?"
"I'll get you another one; don't be dramatic."
"I don't want our son to grow up around violence."
"It wasn't that bad! You're exaggerating everything."

He came up with all sorts of seemingly benevolent phrases to convince me that he had changed, that he could change. But I was determined. I remembered how he had forced us to sleep outside my parents' house and all the times he had assaulted me. I was worried that one day he might raise his hand against

Luisito. I wanted him out of the house, out of our lives. Nothing was going to change my mind.

"You leave right now, or I'll call the police!" I told him.

He grabbed the bag with his clothes and left. It was official. I had ended my relationship with Hector. I had to start from scratch, and I knew it wouldn't be easy, but *I was free.*

Hector followed me everywhere. At first, he tried to win me back. He came to the apartment, brought flowers, and begged me to forgive him. I stayed strong and refused him again and again. Then he tried to convince me that I had made a huge mistake. "No one will want you with a kid! You will never make it as a single mother!"

Even though I was terrified at the idea of not making it on my own, I had found within me enough determination to make it a definite no. However, despite having made such an important decision, I felt lost in life. I didn't know it at the time, but I was going through post-traumatic stress disorder due to the trauma of having lived through violence. Post-traumatic stress disorder is a mental health condition triggered by a frightening situation.

Having lived so many years on alert made it hard for me to fall asleep. It was as if my body was in a constant state of preparation for any attack. I had anxiety and severe distress. Many times, I was paralyzed, blank, immersed in my thoughts. My hair was falling out, and my self-esteem was at rock bottom.

The memories of domestic violence came in flashes. I would be eating breakfast, and suddenly, the memory of Hector accelerating the car would come to me. Or I would be bathing Luisito, and I would suddenly remember how I woke up in a pool of blood. It was involuntary. I did not tell anyone what I had lived through because I felt ashamed of my past and myself. So, I decided to carry this as a big secret.

On one occasion, Hector showed up at the apartment when no one was home. Susy was in her last year of high school and had just left for school. I was with my son when Hector entered the apartment without knocking. Without warning, he came straight to me, grabbed my neck, and with all his strength, lifted me and slammed me to the floor. I lost consciousness. Everything went black, but my sister's screams woke me up.

This time, my sister Susy ran to defend me, shouting furiously at Hector and making him leave our apartment. Although my sister Susy had been timid since she was a child, that moment brought out the fierceness inside her.

Shortly after, I heard that he was in prison. It was finally over—he would never be able to hurt me again. That was the last time I saw Hector.

I was determined to repress all the memories and move forward for my son. Now I had to fight for my future, for my dreams.

MIRACOSTA

After completing the enrollment process at MiraCosta Community College (MCC), I waited for my classes to start. Mom offered to take care of Luisito so that I could continue studying, but he wasn't used to her; for the first two years of his life, he had hardly been around her. The thought of leaving him to go to school made me very anxious. This time, I couldn't take him to school with me. We would be apart for the first time, and that was a strange feeling I tried to push aside until the day to go to my first day of school finally arrived.

Before heading out, I carried Luisito, hugged him tightly, and submerged myself at that moment. I wanted time to stop.

"You are going to miss the bus if you don't leave right now," Mom kept reminding me, her voice hovering around me.

I looked him in his sweet eyes and, with a broken voice, said, "My love, Mom will start going to school. We will have a better future. Someday, I will have a career. We will buy a house, and we will have a puppy. I promise."

I gently kissed him on his forehead, handed him to Mom, and slowly walked out of the apartment. Before closing the door, I looked at him one last time. Luisito was too young to understand; he looked confused. I closed the door and raced down the stairs.

Suddenly, Luisito burst into hysterical crying. I had never heard him cry like that. I stopped and looked up. What kind of mother leaves her child to go to school? I could not leave him like that! I thought as I hesitated and slowly climbed two steps up. Then, I reminded myself that I was going this for him. With a massive lump in my throat, I turned around and ran to the bus station.

In the distance, I could still hear my baby crying; the sound echoed through my mind.

I sat at the back of the bus and cried the entire ride. On top of my guilt for leaving Luisito without a father, I felt that I was abandoning him. I felt selfish for pursuing my dreams. I wanted to go back and hug him. There were many people on the bus, and they all saw me crying, but no one said anything. In that moment of immense weakness, I could have given up. Leaving Luisito crying to go to school was one of the hardest decisions I ever had to make.

I arrived at MCC with my self-esteem at rock bottom. I felt that I didn't belong in this world. The placement test I had completed during the enrollment process indicated that I was below the required English level, which meant that I had to take two non-credit English classes before starting my regular classes. I didn't know how to choose my classes; I didn't know the difference between a bachelor's and a master's degree. I felt lost.

I was a first-generation college student, the daughter of migrant farm workers who had never attended school, much less college. Luckily, the admission office referred me to EOPS (Extended Opportunity Program and Services). This program offers comprehensive academic and support counseling to help students achieve their educational and career goals.

My task at my first EOPS meeting was to create an educational plan and choose my classes. I met with a peer advisor. His first question was if I had already chosen my major. I didn't understand his question, so I asked, "What is a major?" I felt so ashamed of my ignorance.

"A major is the area of study you focus on while pursuing your degree. Think of one of your favorite classes," he explained kindly.

I decided that psychology would be my major during that meeting, and I never changed it.

I met my counselor, Candelaria Urrea Owens, whom I called Candy, in the EOPS program. She was the first Hispanic woman in an academic position I had ever met, an inspiration to me from the first moment—my first role model.

That summer, I took her career-planning class, which taught us to plan our personal and academic goals. Our first activity was to write about our biggest goal in a journal; mine was to graduate from MiraCosta College. Then we were asked to visualize that goal. I closed my eyes, and there I was, wearing a graduation cap and gown, going up the stage to receive my diploma. When I turned to the audience, I saw Luisito in a blue shirt and red tie, smiling while holding a flower bouquet. I was able to see it, to feel it, and my eyes filled with tears. What I didn't know at that time was that when you imagine your future success, your subconscious mind attracts the people and opportunities to make your goals a reality.

I was a full-time student and worked full-time at a chocolate factory earning minimum wage. I packed the product that came out of the machines while on foot all day. It was a repetitive and tedious job. The lady standing next to me told me that she had been doing the same thing every day for fifteen years. I wondered if I could handle doing the same thing for many years.

Mom always told us that her dream was to see us working in an office. Sometimes I would stop in the reception area and watch the administration staff enter and leave their offices. I would close my eyes and visualize myself doing the same thing, entering my office and sitting in front of a desk. I began to wonder what it took to work in an office.

Luisito was three years old at this time. He stayed with Mom while I worked the night shift. Sometimes I would only sleep a couple of hours. The following day, I would get up early to go to school. I don't know where I got the energy.

I was determined to learn English and dreamed of one day speaking it well. I wrote three English words in a red notebook every day. Throughout the day, I would create sentences with that new word. I rented books from the library and googled every word I didn't know. I listened to English music and wrote down the lyrics.

Our final project of Candy's summer class was to give a five-minute presentation about our goals and how we were planning to get there. I was terrified of the thought of speaking in front of my class. I had forgotten the little girl inside me, the one who carried her microphone and gave motivational speeches to her stuffed animals. My self-esteem was so low that I didn't feel worthy of being listened to or looked at, plus I was very self-conscious of my accent. Even though I carried my red notebook everywhere and tried my best to learn English, I still had a thick accent.

Before class, I went to talk to Candy during her office hours. I told her that there was no way I could present, that I was terrified of public speaking. Candy acknowledged my concern but then told me she would stand by my side if necessary but that she would not let my fear stop me from getting a good grade in her class.

Candy stood next to me when I started my presentation. I was so focused that I forgot that she was there. I was so concentrated that I didn't notice when she slowly walked to the other side of the room. When I finished presenting, she smiled and gave me a thumbs up. She was right. I was capable of doing it on my own! My admiration for Candy grew. I admired her so much that I wanted to be exactly like her: professional, successful, and educated.

A NEW PHASE

After summer, fall classes began. While waiting for one of my classes to start, a woman named Elicene casually began talking to me. We sat next to each other in the back of the classroom. She always dressed beautifully; she brought a different bag that matched her outfit every day. She lived in a two-story house and drove her car to school.

Even though Elicene had everything I had never had, she was down to earth. Sometimes, she gifted me beautiful clothes. Thanks to her, little by little, I recovered my self-esteem. We became inseparable. From then on, we chose the same classes every semester to be together. I never told her about my past, though; I was ashamed of it. I tried my best to repress all my memories of domestic abuse.

With Elicene by my side, I got the courage to join the Latina Leadership Network (LLN) club. This club aims to empower Latina women in community college to advance their education and develop leadership skills. Candy was the president of that club, and she was thrilled when I finally decided to join. In the LLN club, I met other Latina students. I was beginning to surround myself with bright people, widening my circle.

At the end of that school year, we took a trip in a van to the annual LLN conference in Visalia, CA. At that conference, I saw other successful Latinas. The first keynote speaker was a business owner, and the second speaker was a writer. Seeing so many Latinas who had overcome challenging circumstances themselves, who had allowed themselves to dream, and who aspired high and succeeded gave me a new perspective. For the first time, I allowed myself to dream big.

On our way back, I sat in the back of the van with Elicene and one of our newest LLN members, who started telling us about how much she wished that her best friend could've been part of this trip. "She couldn't continue with school. She had to move in with her boyfriend after her parents' deportation," she said.

She then began to show us some pictures from her digital camera.

"Look, she's my best friend."
I looked at the picture and shouted, "That's Nallely!"

I couldn't believe how small the world was. After many years, I never thought that I would re-connect with my best friend from high school this way. When I returned to Oceanside, she was no longer in the same neighborhood. I didn't look for her because I thought she would resent that I suddenly stopped talking to her and left for Fresno without saying goodbye.

That day, I got Nallely's phone number and called her. She got so happy when she heard my voice. We spoke for hours! I told her that I had moved back to Oceanside and ended my relationship with Hector three years earlier. I also told her that I was going to graduate from MiraCosta College in a couple of days.

I was twenty-one years old when I finally finished community college. It was graduation day! Everything looked exactly the way I had visualized it. Luisito was wearing a blue dress shirt and a red tie. The graduates were asked to give a one-minute message to their loved ones. From the podium, I could see my family in the front row. I was filled with many emotions.

When it was my turn to speak, I got extremely nervous, but I decided to focus on Luisito.

"Luisito, baby, I love you so much. You are my reason why," I said, wrapped in tears.

He smiled and waved at me.

Then, in stuttering Spanish, I continued, *"Mamá, gracias por todo tu apoyo. Este es solo el comienzo. Voy a continuar con mi licenciatura y luego mi maestría."*

I told Mom that this was just the beginning and that I would continue with my bachelor's degree and then my master's degree. Then I finished by thanking Candy and my professors. The crowd burst into applause, which filled me with excitement.

At graduation, I had an incomparable surprise: Nallely showed up with balloons and a bouquet. She gave me a big hug. She was proud that her friend had graduated from college. The reunion was spectacular and filled my heart.

That day I promised my family and myself that this would not be my last graduation. With the encouragement and help from Candy, I applied to undergraduate school. She wrote the following recommendation letter:

It isn't every day that I meet a student like Erica. In my opinion, as her counselor and professor, I can tell you that she is dedicated, motivated, and passionate. She's the kind of person who, if life gives her lemons, will make lemonade. Her desire to be "someone" in life really impressed me. There is no doubt in my mind that Erica will be successful and that she will pay it forward and be a role model for so many women. She is a people person and is always willing to assist anyone in need.

Candy's words stayed in my heart. I printed her letter and taped it on my wall to look at every day.

Grandpa visited me a week after graduation. I wanted to spoil him, so I invited him for hamburgers. We left the house and headed to my car. Grandpa couldn't believe that his granddaughter had a car and knew how to drive! I put on a Vicente Fernandez CD, and we drove away. I shared with him my plans as we devoured our hamburgers and fries. I showed him my graduation pictures and told him that I was going to continue studying and that one day, I was going to have a career and earn enough money to buy him the boots that he wanted so much. For the first time, my grandfather looked at me in the same way he looked at my brother: with great pride. His face lit up with a smile. I felt fulfilled.

"I will spoil you, *Abuelito*!" I told him before he left. We began to laugh. I can still hear the echo of his laughter.

A couple of weeks after graduation, I went to pick up the mail, and there it was! The acceptance letter from California State University, the same school I had visited during my middle school field trip. I was so excited. My life was taking new directions to places I wouldn't have dared to even dream about just years before. I couldn't wait for the next chapter in my life.

MY WORLD STOPPED

I enrolled at CSUSM as a full-time student. I excitedly counted the days to start my classes. When the day finally arrived, I woke up two hours early and drove twenty minutes east to San Marcos. Life was going better than I had planned.

When I arrived at CSUSM, I went up the stairs and walked around the building. Then I sat on a bench under a tree to look at the breathtaking view. I couldn't believe it! I pulled out my student identification to make sure I wasn't dreaming.

As I walked to my first class, I began to feel nervous. I wondered if the admissions office had made a mistake in accepting me into this school. I sat in the back of the room, not knowing why I felt so insecure but hoping that no one would notice. Candy was no longer there to cheer me up, and Elicene had gotten married, so she wasn't in class with me.

The days passed, and I managed to be a full-time student while working full-time. I became so good at translating from English to Spanish that I was now working as a telephonic translator for workers' compensation. I was in an office setting, sat in front of a desk, and made more than minimum wage.

Luisito had just turned five, but I couldn't understand him when he spoke. Besides his speech problem, he was also having a hard time walking. I thought that maybe the pediatrician was right when he said that perhaps he was too spoiled, and that's why he walked on his tiptoes. He fell whenever he tried to run, and for that reason, we carried him in our arms or pushed him in a stroller. I was a young, inexperienced mother.

At first, I didn't see his slow learning curve as a problem. Not until I began to compare him with other kids his age. I became concerned and took him to his lifelong pediatrician for a physical checkup.

This time, I was able to express my concerns. Luisito's pediatrician referred us to a specialist.

I was scheduled to see the specialist at Rady Children's Hospital in San Diego a couple of days later. He performed multiple tests on Luisito; it was a long and tedious process. After six weeks, I was finally scheduled for the final diagnosis.

I took my mom with me to that appointment. While we were in the waiting room, Luisito fell asleep. Suddenly, they called my name. I asked Mom to stay in the waiting room with Luisito, stood up, and followed the specialist. He carried a folder in his hands as we walked into his office. I sat in front of his desk.

There was a stark silence before he looked me in the eye and said, "Your child has cerebral palsy."

"Cerebral palsy?" I asked, confused.

The specialist explained to me, "Cerebral palsy affects a child's motor and neurological development." He continued by telling me that my son might have a mental disability, which might have been why he did not speak well.

"Your son will never walk like other children."

As he described the many things Luisito may not be able to do, my heart started pounding so hard it felt like it was going to burst out of my chest.

I wanted to know why my son had cerebral palsy, so I asked the specialist, "What causes cerebral palsy?"

The specialist gave me many explanations, but as soon as he said, "brain injury during pregnancy." My world stopped.

My hands started shaking, and my heart started pounding faster than ever. All the memories of domestic abuse began to flash through my mind. I remembered how Hector sat on my stomach, how he pushed me, and how I hit my belly on the corner of the bed.

"Erica, did you ever get hit in the stomach during pregnancy?

I didn't answer his question; I stayed quiet. The neurologist continued talking. I could see his lips moving in slow motion, but I could no longer hear him. If this was a nightmare, I wanted to wake up right then and there. I got up and stormed out of his office without saying anything.

When my mom asked me what was wrong, I couldn't tell her anything. I just told her that we had to leave. I was afraid she would blame me. I felt very guilty.

We were one hour away from home, and there was a lot of traffic. My eyes were fixed on the road. The specialist's words echoed through my head, and memories of the past with it. Something changed in me that day. I began to fill with hatred toward Hector. All the anger I had repressed toward him exploded inside of me. The veins in my knuckles popped as I squeezed the wheel. I had an immense lump in my throat, but I hadn't dared cry in front of the specialist, let alone in front of my mother.

As soon as we arrived at our apartment, I carried Luisito to our room and laid him on his bed. I caressed his hair until he fell asleep. From the moment the doctor gave me the diagnosis, I had been holding back the urge to cry.

"Forgive me, Luisito. I didn't know how to take care of you," I finally said.

I couldn't hold it anymore. My legs collapsed, and I threw myself on the floor and crept into a fetal position. I cried like never before. Never in my life had I felt so much pain, guilt, and hate at the same time. I thought my life would get better after I left Hector, that he would never be able to hurt me again. I was so wrong.

That was the beginning of many months of depression. I cried myself to sleep every night. I started skipping classes. Sometimes, I wouldn't get out of bed, and I stayed submerged in negative thoughts. I blamed myself for putting up with Hector, not having left sooner, and not protecting my baby.

Luisito was referred to physical therapy and speech therapy. I enrolled him in a special school with other kids with speech problems. A bus picked him up every morning to take him to school. I took him to his therapies twice a week. I barely had the energy to continue. I felt deep inside that I had destroyed my son's life.

What good had all that effort done if he was never going to be proud of me, I wondered. I thought I was being punished for leaving my son without a father, so I asked for forgiveness and begged for a miracle.

Months passed, but I no longer thought I had any options. My self-esteem plummeted again. I could no longer see the light at the end of the tunnel. I was exhausted by life and didn't have the emotional tools to manage my conflicts.

I tried to keep it a secret that I was sunk. I started drinking alcohol habitually, locking myself in the bathroom so no one would see me. I started partying wildly and attracting toxic people into my life. I went out to clubs so the sound of the music could drown out the voices inside me trying to destroy me. The alcohol numbed my pain, but I would wake up feeling worse the next day.

I neglected my entire first semester at CSUSM. My grades dropped so low that I failed all my classes. At the end of that school year, I received a letter stating that I had been academically disqualified from CSUSM. I read that letter several times. I couldn't believe it. My God! I felt I had let everyone down: my parents, Luisito, Mr. Lee, Candy, and myself. With tears in my eyes, I peeled Candy's recommendation letter from my wall and put it in a drawer.

The dream of getting a higher education had ended. My will to live and my optimism were gone. For the first time in my life, I just gave up.

CHANGE IS POSSIBLE

Many things happened shortly after graduating from MiraCosta, Susy moved in with her boyfriend and went to live in Tijuana. Luis spent most of his time with his girlfriend and his friends. Dad's job gave him different assignments throughout Northern California, and he was away from home on week days. He got home Friday night and left Sunday afternoon. At home, Mom constantly reproached me. She thought that I had just taken a break from school and surrounded myself with toxic people. She never asked what was going on with me. I kept all the pain to myself.

One Saturday morning, Mom opened the bathroom door and found me sleeping among empty cans of beer. I woke up to her screams; she scolded me the entire day. She was upset with me, but more with Dad because he stayed quiet the whole time she scolded me.

The following day, Dad woke up earlier than usual and knocked on my door. "Hey, let's grab breakfast at McDonald's," he whispered.

Dad bought me a breakfast meal. We sat inside the restaurant, and he gently unwrapped half of my McMuffin and handed it to me. I was a little girl the last time Dad sat and talked to me. Now I was an adult, a stranger to him. He tried so hard to talk to me, but he didn't know how. We both stayed quiet. Then he looked out the window, submerged in his thoughts, and his eyes filled with tears.

"Dad, I'm sorry," I stuttered.
"Little turtle, we have all made mistakes," Dad replied.

After months of guilt and mourning for my son's diagnosis, that day I realized that I could no longer keep this to myself. Dad was the first person I told about Luisito's diagnosis and how I felt. He never scolded me, he never judged me—he truly cared. That weekend, Dad didn't leave. He switched to a lower-paying job that didn't require him to travel.

I deactivated all my social media accounts, changed my phone number, and cut my long hair. I stopped partying and drinking, but I still felt empty inside. One night, while my family slept, I sat on the edge of my bed; I could look out the window from there. I stared up at the dark sky for hours. "I surrender," I finally said, crying. That night, I vowed to learn to accept what I couldn't change.

I became closer than ever to my family. They all helped me take care of Luisito: Mom and Dad took him to McDonald's every weekend, Susy took him to the park, and my brother played with him.

Luisito continued receiving speech therapy and physical therapy twice a week. After several months, he could now say short phrases and even write his name. After a year of treatment, he could finally run without falling.

One afternoon, we visited my grandparents in Tijuana. Since they had moved to Oaxaca and only came to Tijuana twice a year, we got very excited every time they came. When we arrived, Grandpa came out of their house, very happy to welcome us. His white shirt was splattered with salsa. With that joy, he led Susy and me into the kitchen. On the table, there was a *molcajete*, and everything was splashed with salsa.

Yes, he was cooking! *Abuelito*! The one who used to say that cooking was only for women was now splashed with tomato sauce. My sister and I turned to look at each other and laughed; we were very happy. He had the happiest smile ever and said to us: "Look, my dear granddaughters, I'm making sauce for your grandmother. I've changed."

That moment was magical. It was one of the most beautiful scenes I remember of my grandparents. That day, my grandfather said that he would not be a "macho" anymore. that he was going to help Grandma and take care of her. That was the last time I saw him. A few weeks later, Grandfather died unexpectedly. His appendix burst, and he couldn't get to the hospital in time.

The memory that stayed in my heart is of a candid and wonderful grandfather. Every drop of tomato on his shirt represented a desire to change. And that's what he did at the end of his life. We all have that right: the right to improve.

One morning I was getting Luisito ready for school, in a hurry as usual since I was running late for work. I sat him on the edge of the bed and knelt down to tie his shoelaces. Suddenly, I felt his tiny fingers caress my hair. I looked up to find Luisito gazing at me. With his two little hands, he grabbed my face and asked, "Mommy, do you already have a career? Remember you used to say that one day you were going to have a career."

I thought I had imagined it. It was the first time I had heard him speak so clearly.

"What did you say?" I asked, still believing that I had probably hallucinated it.

"Mommy, remember that every night you used to tell me that you were going to have a career and that we were going to have a house and a puppy? Do you already have a career and that's why you don't go to school anymore?"

I was so excited that I felt my heart racing. My eyes filled with tears, and I hugged him tightly. "Do you still remember?" I asked him.

"Yes, Mommy," he said.
"You can talk clearly, my love!" I said through tears. "Mom just took a little break, but I promise I will go back. I will make you proud of me."

At that very moment, I decided I was going to resume my studies.

RESUMING MY STUDIES

My son's words had given me back the hope and desire to fight for another chance. That day, I didn't go to work. Instead, I headed to CSUSM. Tears of joy kept falling from my eyes on my way there. As soon as I arrived, I went to the admissions office. I told them that I had been academically disqualified and asked what I had to do to be a student there again. The requirements were not easy—I had to take one semester at a community college to demonstrate that I could complete a semester successfully.

I enrolled as a full-time student at MiraCosta College and took classes to develop my skills in office administration. At the end of that semester, we had a special guest from a communication club.

"Hello, my name is Henry. I am a member of Toastmasters."

That was the first time I heard of Toastmasters, an internationally recognized communication and leadership organization.

At the end of that semester at MiraCosta College, I completed all my classes. I demonstrated academic success, and CSUSM gave me another chance!

I was 24 years old when I was re-admitted to CSUSM in 2014. I dedicated all my heart and soul to making up for the lost time when I returned. Sometimes I wondered if I could obtain a university degree if someone with the same background had done it before. I wanted some assurance or inspiration. I started looking for stories on Google or something to inspire me or give me hope. In one of the searches, I read this statistic: "Less than two percent of teenage mothers get a college degree by the age of thirty." It put a lump in my throat. I reread that statistic a couple of times and then said to myself, "Erica, you are going to be part of that two percent." That became my mantra.

Even with my busy schedule, I managed to obtain good grades during those two years. Every

Saturday, I took Luisito to school with me, and we spent the entire day at the library. I had a frantic pace of life, working and studying full-time. But for Luisito, I was more determined than ever. Giving up was no longer an option.

PART
4

PART

I

FINDING FORGIVENESS

Before my last semester of undergrad, I received news that my grandmother, Regina, was very ill. I traveled to Oaxaca to visit her. The night I arrived, I slept by her side. It was midnight, but I could see her gray hair and her wrinkled eyes in the moonlight. I had always wondered what my dear grandmother thought of me.

In my culture, leaving a husband is the worst thing that a woman could do. When I ended my relationship with Hector, I was deeply criticized by the people that knew my family. My grandmother never gave her opinion; she never criticized me. As I was submerged in my thoughts, she suddenly opened her eyes.

"Granddaughter, you can't sleep?" she asked me in her Mixteco dialect.

I gathered courage. "Granny, do you think I was wrong to have left my son without a father? Was I wrong to have left Hector?" I asked her.

She stared into my eyes, and with a depth I had never seen in her, she said, "I wish I had been as brave as you."

I hugged her. "Thank you, Grandma," I whispered to her and began to cry.

In one instant, her words freed me of those old beliefs that I had carried and that had weighed so heavily upon me. She liberated me of immense guilt and agony. I understood that I had done the right thing to protect my son and myself. Together, we broke the family chain, those old customs, and traditions. Through me, Grandma was able to see a new generation of women in her family before passing away. I will forever carry the beautiful and meaningful memory of that moment with me.

I returned to continue with my last semester of school. One weekend, without planning it, I went to a bookstore in search of a self-help book, but I wasn't sure where to start. I walked up and down the aisles. Suddenly, a bright orange book, *God Never Blinks* by Regina Brett caught my attention, so I bought the book. In the first chapters, the author talked about the importance of forgiving people who have hurt you. Living with hatred and resentment toward someone is poison for yourself, and it is also useless because the other person does not even know what you are feeling. I thought that maybe I could forgive someone who had hurt me, but how could I forgive someone who had hurt my son? I was clinging to the idea that Hector had hurt my son.

Since I had found out that Luisito had cerebral palsy, the only thing I had done was to hate him with all my heart, and that didn't do me any good. Hating him was a huge burden, and that hatred and resentment kept me from being happy. Forgiving was not an easy decision, but I decided to do it because I deserved peace. For the first time, I put myself in his shoes and felt sorry for him.

On a piece of paper, I wrote this letter:

I know that you love Luisito very much and that your intention was not to hurt him. I know that you suffered a lot in your childhood and used drugs to escape, and although you never told me what happened and maybe I will never understand it, I know that you grew up without love. I have no idea what you suffered that made you choose to use drugs from the age of thirteen. I saw all the scars on your back and your head. I don't want to hate you anymore. I don't want to curse you anymore. I want you to be well, and I want to tell you that I sincerely forgive you.

I want you to be happy.

Writing that letter was a huge step toward my healing, the first big step toward my resilience. I let go of grudges and desires of revenge; instead, I felt immense peace. I freed myself. Hector could no longer affect my life; I could finally move forward.

During my last semester in college, our professor told us that our final project would consist of a twenty-five-minute presentation in which we had to share our educational journey.

"We all have a story to tell," she said.

I was still afraid of public speaking, but I remembered the Toastmasters guest. I was determined to pass her class and confront that fear. That's when I decided to look for a local Toastmasters.

I felt extremely nervous as I walked to my first Toastmasters meeting. When I entered the room, I was warmly greeted by the members, who were all white. I felt very intimidated—my heart was pounding. I sat in the back of the room; I was planning to run out as soon as they got distracted. I was terrified!

The meeting was divided into parts. The first part was the "Table Topics" section. This section is intended to help members develop their ability to quickly organize their thoughts and respond to impromptu questions. All the guests were invited to participate, but I refused.

I regretted coming to the meeting, but I was already there; I just had to wait for the second part of the meeting to end. This section was reserved for prepared speeches. The first speaker was introduced as a speech contestant. I hadn't seen her when I came in, but when she stood up to share her speech, I noticed she was Hispanic. Immediately, all my attention went to her as if she were a mirror in which I could see myself.

That was the first time I heard Dora's story of resilience. She had a child with disabilities, and in her speech, she told us about the moment she was given her daughter's diagnosis. Her speech touched me and at the same time inspired me so much that, no matter how hard I tried, I couldn't stop the tears from falling. In her speech, Dora taught me that you can be strong and vulnerable at the same time.

After listening to Dora's speech, I decided to join Toastmasters. As soon as I got home, I wrote in my journal, "One day, I will share my story in front of fifty people." As I wrote that, I felt that I was exaggerating. I erased that number and wrote twenty-five people. *Erica, you need to be more realistic*, I thought. At that moment, the most important thing was to face my fear of public speaking, but I also desperately wanted to grow, and to do that, I had to allow myself to feel uncomfortable. Growth is obtained by walking beyond your comfort zone.

THE ERICA FROM THE PAST

My life was at full speed. There were days when I slept for only a few hours. I didn't eat well, exercise, or drink enough water. We all know that the body has a limit, and mine had reached it. The morning of January 1, 2017, a sudden pain began on the right side of my lower abdomen. The pain worsened that night; it was sharp and stabbing. I didn't sleep at all.

My parents had left for Tijuana on New Year's Eve, so I asked my sister to take Luisito and me to them the next day. We got to the house in Tijuana that afternoon, and I told my parents that maybe I had eaten something that upset my stomach. I was in so much pain that Mom became very concerned. She wanted to take me to the hospital, but our neighbor offered to help. She gave me an injection that immediately put me to sleep. The pain was no longer there the following day. After two days of not being able to eat, I was starving. Mom prepared me oatmeal for breakfast. I threw up everything when I finished eating, and the sharp pain returned.

Susy and I had to return to Oceanside. Our jobs were waiting for us. Before leaving Tijuana, I asked my parents to take care of Luisito and assured them that I was feeling better. Susy left for work, and I stayed in the apartment to rest. I developed a fever, felt weak, and collapsed in the living room.

A burst appendix is a severe and potentially life-threatening medical problem. When the appendix gets blocked, bacteria builds up inside, which causes pain and swelling. If not treated quickly, the appendix can burst and spread infection throughout the body. That's what happened to me.

I wasn't answering my dad's calls, so he got very concerned and returned to Oceanside. He found me on the living room floor and took me straight to the emergency room. Three days had passed between when my appendix burst and when I was taken to the ER. All my organs had become infected, and I required immediate surgery to remove the appendix and treat the infection.

When I woke up from the surgery, I saw Luisito crying by my bed and my whole family standing behind him. They visited me every day that I was in the hospital. When I was discharged, the doctor said I could not eat solid food, only soups. As soon as I got home, my brother brought me several soups from my favorite restaurant. My family helped me get up because it was difficult to walk. I stayed in bed for weeks, and my parents, siblings, and Luisito took care of me.

When I was bedridden recovering, I often dreamed of that cold night outside the house in Fresno. I could see the sixteen-year-old Erica, the Erica of the past, crying while holding Luisito in her arms. I tried to talk to her from behind the gate, but she couldn't see me, much less hear me. "Erica, it's going to be okay!" I kept telling her over and over again. I wanted so badly to hug her, but the bars were so high that I couldn't get close to her. I didn't understand why I had to remember her that way, let alone at that moment when I was so weak.

I'm not sure if it was the Oxycodone that I was prescribed, but my dreams became strange. I dreamed I was finishing a speech in front of an audience, and I got a standing ovation. Suddenly, I heard distant applause that woke me up. It was strange because I could hear them clearly, but no one was around me. It was like an auditory hallucination. That vision accompanied me during my recovery, without my being able to give it a logical explanation. While I was in such bad condition, I was able to rethink things and realize that I needed to live a more relaxed life and not demand so much of myself. I learned to value my health.

It took me six weeks to recover, but when I did, I continued with my last semester of undergrad and returned to Toastmasters. The day before my twenty-five-minute presentation final, in which I had to share my educational journey and background, I already had a presentation ready. I started looking through old boxes of photos; I wanted to add a picture of my grandparents. That's when I came across a photo of sixteen-year-old Erica. In that photo, I was carrying my baby in my arms—it was the day Luisito was born. I grabbed the picture and stared at it for a few minutes. I remembered how she felt: very lonely in her journey. She was always looking for a story that would give her hope, but she never found it. Then I hugged the photo and started to cry.

Forgive me for blaming you. It was not your fault. Forgive me for being ashamed of you, for wanting to forget you. You were so brave. I have never told you this, but I am proud of you. I promise that I will share your story. I will do it in your honor.

The last step for my healing process was to forgive myself. For the first time, I reconnected with my past and made peace with it. This day I promised to love and respect myself. The experience of being between life and death made me completely lose my fear. I plucked up the courage, and that night, I started a new presentation.

The next day, I had the class in front of me. I was so nervous that I had to ask our professor to turn off the lights, and then I began. I talked about my grandparents' customs, about my childhood, about my parents' long days in the fields, about the struggle to settle in the United States. I spoke about Hector, his abuse, and all the violence he committed against me during our relationship and my pregnancy. I talked about my son's diagnosis, my past depression, my alcoholism, how I almost lost the opportunity to attend this school. I shared all my life in the raw.

At the end of the presentation, I felt like hundreds of wild birds had been uncaged in my chest; they flew out, bringing me back to life. I could not see the students' faces because the light was off. There was only total silence, not a murmur. I told the teacher I had finished, that we could turn on the light. Then, when the light broke through the blackness in the room and illuminated the faces of my classmates, I saw that the teacher and several students had tears in their eyes. They all began to applaud, telling me that they never imagined that I had gone through something like that. It was true that I didn't show my wounds or go around with a victim mentality, so it would have been hard to guess that I came from such a complicated place in life. Some of the girls in the class said to me, "Wow, you just inspired me. I went through something similar."

The level of sincerity and intensity in all the presentations that followed mine increased. After me, everyone started to let loose. They dared to tell their story like this, in the raw, instead of telling general stories like they had previously. I inspired people to heal, to tell their stories. I shared my story for the second time with my Toastmasters Club. It was the first speech I gave at my club.

I discovered that having been ashamed of my story, I was hurting myself. My life came full circle by letting go of it and seeing what it could generate in other people. That's how I forged my destiny. I was selected as the commencement speaker at the end of that semester. The girl who had been academically disqualified a few years back was now chosen to give the graduation speech in front of thousands of people.

When I told my Toastmasters group that I had been chosen as the keynote speaker for the graduation ceremony, they celebrated and helped me prepare. They all became my mentors, my second family.

DÉJÀ VU

Graduation day arrived. I woke up very early and put on my graduation gown and the cap I had decorated a few days before. On the top, it said: *We made it, Luisito, 2%*. Officially, I was part of the two percent of teenage mothers with a college degree. My parents were very proud that I was graduating college with a bachelor's degree in psychology. I was the first woman in our family to get a degree.

That day, the university assigned me a chair which had a sign that said, "Keynote Speaker." I was filled with many emotions and nerves. When my name was called, I walked to the podium, stopped in front of the stairs, looked up to the sky and said, *"Abuelita*, this speech is for you. I hope you are proud of your granddaughter." I walked up to the podium on shaky legs and gave the following speech:

Faculty, family, friends, and fellow graduates, good morning! One of my professors once said, "We all have a story to tell." She instructed everyone in the classroom to create a twenty-five-minute presentation and share their own stories. That assignment made me reflect and remember the circumstances that brought me here.

Today, I would like to share with all of you a little bit about myself. When I was fifteen years old, I found out that I was pregnant. After dropping out of high school, I moved to Fresno with my boyfriend and lived under domestic abuse for many years. My life took a turn the night my baby's father forced me and my baby to sleep outside. In the midst of my despair, two memories came to mind.

The first was when I was fourteen years old. My mother would take me to work with her in the tomato fields. Once, when I told her that I was tired, she said, "This is our life; the people who have a good life are the ones who have a good education."

The second memory was the first time I visited Cal State San Marcos during a school field trip. I was impressed to see such a big school. I walked around the buildings and wondered if it was even possible for someone like me to become a student here.

After graduating from high school, I returned to Oceanside and ended the abusive relationship. My biggest goal at the time was to become a student at that school with the big buildings. In 2012, I enrolled at Cal State San Marcos. I was very nervous but excited to finally be here.

Like many of you, I had many excuses to give up. I am a single mother, a first-generation college student. English is my second language. And sometimes, I had to work full-time while being a full-time student, but giving up was no longer an option. I used to whisper to myself over and over again, "Less than two percent of teenage mothers get a college degree, less than two percent. Erica, you're going to be in that two percent."

We are all here because we did not give up. Now it's time for us to set new goals and to keep moving forward. Class of 2017, when it comes to your dreams, be as persistent as you can. Confront your fears and never, ever doubt yourself. Congratulations, class of 2017; we did it!

At the end of the speech, everyone stood up and started shouting and clapping, and at that moment, I realized this scene was exactly what I had seen many times in my dream when I was bedridden and trying to recover. I would wake up to the sound of applause. Was it simply a premonition? There are things in life we cannot explain . . . the most magical things . . .

After I gave the speech, I was put in front to lead all the graduates out. There were so many people around me, and I saw my brother in the distance looking at me with such pride. He had a huge smile on his face and was waiting for me with open arms. I went toward him with a hurried step. We gave each other a hug so tight that he almost lifted me up. I got a lump in my throat because physical affection is something we had never given each other. Although my brother was always treated differently, he never felt superior. On the contrary, he always wanted something better for his sisters. My brother has always inspired us and pushed us to be better. His example has been key in my life.

And so, in 2017, at the age of twenty-seven, I finally graduated. In celebration of my achievement, my family proudly threw a last-minute party in our back yard. As I was getting ready in my sister's room, I heard my brother entering the house with his friends.

I heard the voice of a gentleman who said, "This gift card is for your sister." "You give it to her," my brother replied.

"But I don't know her," replied the stranger.

Wrapped in curiosity, I went into the living room and saw my brother's friend for the first time. We stared at each other, then he approached me with a wide smile. That man before me filled me with confidence. A few weeks earlier, my brother had run into an old friend from high school, whom he had not seen for many years. They had met each other just on time, just before my graduation, and so my brother brought José Manuel along to the celebration.

My brother introduced us. "Erica, this is my friend, José Manuel."

"Nice to meet you," I said, smiling and gently grabbing the card from his hand.

"The pleasure is mine," replied José Manuel.

"Starbucks! How did you know I love coffee?"

That day, we danced, and it was instant chemistry. It seemed as if we had known each other forever, although we had never met before. From that moment to this day, we are still together. I have experienced a healthy relationship for the first time, thanks to this man.

I achieved my goals, and the love of my life appeared. It was as if good things brought more good things. As if, by opening yourself energetically to all the good that can happen, things will settle on their own. I was already very prepared for a new relationship, significantly healed. My life was already in order. José entered my life at the right time; it seemed a thing of fate. They say that things happen when you least expect them. José Manuel is, for Luisito, the father figure he never had. He cares for him, loves him, and is a good role model for him.

As a result of my graduation speech, the university newspaper wrote an article about me titled "From Teen Mom to College Graduate." In the article, they told my story and talked about my speech, my life, and how I got to be the speaker for that graduating class. A few days after my graduation, I received an email from the person who would change my life: K. Ryan.

UNEXPECTED GIFT

K. Ryan is the pseudonym of a person who wished to remain anonymous. She read the article "From Teen Mom to College Graduate" that the CSUSM News Center wrote about me. It caught her attention. In that article, I mentioned that I was planning to pursue a master's degree. Of course, I did not have the financial resources to do so.

K. Ryan's email said: *I read the article that was published about you. This is my number; there is something important I want to talk to you about. I'll be waiting for your call.*

I didn't think twice. I called her right then and there and said, "Hi, my name is Erica. I got your email."

In our conversation, she told me that my story had moved her very much and that she wanted to finance my master's degree. My mind didn't know how to process this. I didn't know how to react, so I simply said, "Thank you."

I was a little scared because, in any case, I did not know this person. It could even be a fake email or a prank. José Manuel gave me the idea of meeting her in person to see if everything was real. That's how we met at a Starbucks. The first thing I asked her was, "Are you really going to finance my master's degree?"

"Yes," she replied. "You just tell me when you finish the application process, and I'll send the check directly to the university. And please, I want my anonymity to be preserved."
"But . . . why do you want to do this for me?" I asked, still confused.

To which she replied, as if she had seen through my soul, "Because I know that you are going to pay it forward."

Her appearance in my life was like a miracle. That person gave me an unexpected gift, and thanks to her altruism, I was able to take the first step toward an even greater goal. A couple of weeks after meeting with her I started my graduate studies at San Diego State University (SDSU). My new goal was to obtain a master's degree in Education with a concentration in counseling. Every day, I worked very hard to be a brilliant student.

Luisito was eleven years old when I started graduate school. He always told me, "Mom, I'm so proud of you." Luisito defied the specialist's diagnosis and became an exemplary student. Not only did he walk, but he also ran, skated, and even surfed. Every six months, he received injections in the backs of his legs, which allowed him to walk like other children.

José Manuel always accompanied me to his appointments. He and I have built a beautiful relationship. Finally, my stormy past was behind me. Now, I had someone by my side who supported me unconditionally.

In April 2019, three weeks before my graduation, I wanted to surprise my mom, so I put on my graduation cap and gown and walked into her room with a stellar appearance. With the enthusiasm of someone who had just fulfilled a dream I had been working on for some time, I said, "*Mamita*, we made it! I am going to receive a master's degree!"

My mom, who is a very strong woman who I have rarely seen cry, broke down and started crying. She repeated over and over again, "All those hours working in the fields, all the sacrifices, were worth it. I'm so proud of you." Seeing your mother cry with happiness over an accomplishment of yours, and more so, a mother who is reluctant to express her emotions, fills the whole soul.

At that moment, I thought I wanted to do something special for my parents, a tribute, something that we could carry with us forever as a symbol of this achievement. That's when I came up with the idea of taking the graduation pictures in one of the fields where my parents had worked long hours to give us an education. The field represented a lot to me—it was where it all began, my first memory. Also, I had decided to go back to school thanks to the memory of the summer when Mom took me to work in the fields, of her advice that day: "If you want to have a better life, you have to study."

I hired a photographer to take the graduation pictures in the field a few weeks before the official graduation ceremony. My mom, dad, and I went to the strawberry field together. Oh, it was beautiful! That day, we remembered our entire journey, watching life pass before our eyes like a secret movie that only we knew about. I felt like I had crossed a generational sea in just an instant. It was not so many years ago. Now, the daughter of two farm workers who couldn't read or write was going to receive a master's degree from SDSU. The struggle, effort, and sacrifice had been worth it.

The pictures turned out beautifully, so at midnight on May 13, 2019, I shared them on my social media accounts and on the Facebook group Latinas Think Big, a community of entrepreneurial and professional women who support each other's empowerment. In the publication, I put the following message: "With much affection, I dedicate my master's degree to my parents. Their sacrifices to come to this country to give us a better future were worth it."

When I woke up the next morning, I simply could not believe it. The photo had over two thousand likes on the Latinas Think Big Facebook group and had been shared hundreds of times. That same day, a local news channel met me for an interview. How could it be that, from one day to the next, I had gone from being a completely unknown person to being interviewed by the media? In that interview, I expressed my desire to inspire other students and my son, Luisito. I ended the interview with these words as I held my son's hand: "My son represents a new generation. He will have more opportunities, and I will be there to tell him that it is possible. That he belongs. All those things that I never heard."

My family and friends couldn't believe it! We were going to be on the local news! We couldn't wait for the report that evening. Everyone teased me, "Erica, you are now famous!" I couldn't believe that I was on the local channel. I just didn't know how to process it.

On the official day of my graduation, I arrived a little late, and on the way, I saw that I had many calls and messages from numbers that I didn't recognize. When I arrived at the entrance of the auditorium, several reporters were waiting for me. They asked many questions. "How does it feel to know that your photo went viral?" I couldn't even move toward the graduation site. I couldn't believe it. Anyone would have thought I was famous! I told them that, I would give them an interview as soon as the graduation was over.

"Did my photo really go viral?" I asked myself. I grabbed my phone and googled my name.

I couldn't believe it! It was true that the photograph was all over the news in the U.S. How was it possible since I had only been in the local news? Other news outlets had picked up and circulated the image. At that moment, I was the representation of the American dream for many immigrants.

At graduation, when they called my name, Erica Alfaro, my legs were shaking. I had fulfilled the biggest dream of my life. I repeated to myself many times, "It's not a dream, Erica, it's happening. It's not a dream, it's not a dream!" It did, indeed, seem like a dream because I had dreamt it thousands of times. But this time, it was real! I had visualized myself there many times, and now the dream was coming true. "You really did it!" I said to myself.

After my graduation, we celebrated at home. That night, I still couldn't believe what was happening. The photo went even more viral. My phone was ringing off the hook. I tried my best to focus only on my graduation party. But the next day, I finally processed everything that was going on. In just a day, I had received thousands of messages on social media. I felt intimidated—I wanted to hide, to ignore all the calls and all the emails—but then I read some of the messages I'd received on my social media accounts. There really were thousands of them. All of them touched my heart.

And that's when I realized that it wasn't about me anymore, so I made the decision that I was going to take all the interviews. Every two hours, a reporter came to my house, and for a whole week, I shared my story non-stop. I was featured on the front cover of the *Toastmaster* international magazine as a prominent speaker! And to think that at the first meeting, I wanted to run away.

Then I was contacted by CNN. They interviewed me at my house, and after that, the picture went even more viral. Now my story made headlines around the world. Kamala Harris, the first woman vice president of the United States, shared my story on her social media account with the following message: *Erica's Story is America's Story: a story of hope, determination and finding her American dream.*

A few days after, I received the following letter:

Dear *Erica,*

Congratulations on your graduation from San Diego State University. Graduate degrees are no small feat, and I am confident that this incredible accomplishment will be just one of many proud moments for you and your family.

The sacrifice your parents made to give their children a better future is the epitome of the American dream. Your accomplishments will serve as a guide for future first-generation students seeking higher education.

I wish you the best of success in everything you do.

Sincerely,

Kamala D. Harris

The experience of going viral taught me that it's important to be prepared because you never know when an opportunity might come along. If I had not gone to Toastmasters, I would not have been able to speak in front of a camera. I would not have been able to give an interview, let alone share my story in front of big audiences.

HARVESTING DREAMS

I started telling my story at several community colleges. A few weeks after my graduation and my photos going viral, I received a call from the founder of Vision Young Leaders Academy, a youth mentoring organization in Ventura County. Most of the members of this organization were Hispanic middle school students.

"I'm white," she said in that call. "I try to inspire them, but they can't see themselves in me. I'm sure you can inspire them."

I thought my story was only going to be shared with adults. I didn't feel that my story could be an inspiration for younger girls since my life was not perfect. But the woman was so insistent that I decided to accept her invitation.

As I shared my story with the members of Vision Young Leaders Academy, I could see how the girls became teary-eyed. When I finished sharing, one of them raised her hand and said, "Now I understand. Hard moments in life are not there to stop us, but to make us stronger. The secret is not to give up."

That touched my heart. After that speech, all the girls ran to ask for my autograph. Me? Who would have thought that I could be someone's role model! That I could inspire someone to fight for their dreams. I ended up becoming the person that I had always looked for. The role model that I always looked for turned out to be me.

My story is the story of many immigrants who come to this country with the hope of a better life, pursuing the American Dream. The young woman I met at one of the first conferences made me see why my story and my photo had gone viral in such away. By sharing my story, I was planting a seed of hope in other people; I was harvesting dreams. I came from parents who harvested the fields, and thanks to their efforts, I was now able to harvest dreams for others.

My identity is inevitably that of an immigrant, and although this has generated both external and internal conflicts, over time I learned there are few things as enriching as growing up in two different cultures. The fields have always been a place related to my parents and a starting point from which to dream. My parents were my best examples of persistence, effort, and sacrifice. They never complained about the hard work. Even though they never went to school and couldn't read or write, they were able to instill in their three children the importance of having a good education. My beloved grandparents were the most beautiful thing in our childhood; from them, we received so much love. At the end of their days, they taught me that change is possible.

I feel very fortunate to have my brother Luis and my sister Susy. They were the best part of my childhood; they always tried their best to protect me. They are my best friends and my inspiration.

My dreams were achieved thanks to the angels and organizations that crossed my path to make the impossible possible. Mr. Lee guided me to greater goals, Candy gave me the tools to achieve those goals, and K. Ryan gave me the gift of graduate education. EOPS gave me the resources to succeed in college, the LLN club inspired me to dream big, and Toastmasters helped me discover my passion for public speaking.

Luisito, my son, is the reason I fought for my dreams. How could I tell him to pursue his dreams if I didn't pursue mine? My biggest dreams had finally come true. To make my son proud of me, to get a career, buy a house, and get our puppies. And as a bonus, to marry the love of my life.

As the daughter of migrant farm workers, a survivor of domestic violence, a teenage mother, and a first-generation college student, I can tell you that all my adversities were stones on the road with which I built my palace.

If you are going through a difficult time in your life and feel like giving up, don't do it! The worst kind of defeat is to give up. My journey wasn't easy, but I wouldn't change anything at all because I rose from my ashes like a phoenix, discovering an even stronger version of myself. Perhaps that is the key to everything: to not be afraid of pain or failure. You can use your adversities as an excuse to stop, or you can use them as a reason to keep moving forward.

I want to thank my Erica of the past, despite feeling small and incapable of fulfilling big dreams. Thank you for resisting, for continuing, for fighting!

ABOUT THE AUTHOR

Erica Alfaro is the proud daughter of migrant farm workers, born in the heart of the central valley farmlands in Fresno and raised in Tijuana, Mexico. As such, her heart's passion is to advocate for the rights of workers in this sector. She is currently part of the human resources department of one of the biggest fields in the area of North County, California.

Erica is a business owner, keynote speaker, and educational advocate. She earned her master's in Education with a concentration in Counseling as well as a Mental Health Recovery and Trauma-informed Care certificate from San Diego State University. Erica received a bachelor's degree in Psychology from California State University San Marcos and an office professional administrative certificate from MiraCosta Community College.

Erica focuses her spare time on advancing the opportunities of other women and migrant children by giving them hope and inspiring them to dream big. She has joined forces with several non-profit organizations that help domestic-violence survivors and first-generation college students as well as an orphanage in Tijuana.

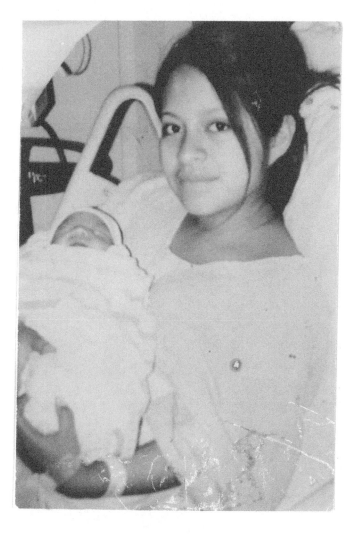

Erica con su bebé Luisito en brazos
Febrero 27 2006

KAMALA D. HARRIS
CALIFORNIA

UNITED STATES SENATE
WASHINGTON, D.C. 20510

June 12, 2019

Dear Erica,

Congratulations on your graduation from San Diego State University. Graduate degrees are no small feat and I trust that this incredible milestone will be just one of many proud moments for you and your family.

The sacrifice your parents made to give their children a better future is the epitome of the American dream. Your accomplishments will serve as a guiding light for future first generation students pursuing higher education.

I wish you the very best success in everything that you do.

Sincerely,

Kamala D. Harris
United States Senator